BUSHWHACKED

DR. MUHAMMED NIAZ

BUSHWHACKED

iUniverse books may be ordered through booksellers or by contacting:

iUniverse
1663 Liberty Drive
Bloomington, IN 47403
www.iuniverse.com
844-349-9409

Because of the dynamic nature of the Internet, any web addresses or links contained in this book may have changed since publication and may no longer be valid. The views expressed in this work are solely those of the author and do not necessarily reflect the views of the publisher, and the publisher hereby disclaims any responsibility for them.

Any people depicted in stock imagery provided by Getty Images are models, and such images are being used for illustrative purposes only.
Certain stock imagery © Getty Images.

ISBN: 978-1-6632-2031-8 (sc)
ISBN: 978-1-6632-2033-2 (hc)
ISBN: 978-1-6632-2032-5 (e)

Library of Congress Control Number: 2022914048

Print information available on the last page.

iUniverse rev. date: 07/18/2022

PREFACE

I was working in my office when my office secretary asked if I could take a call from the vice president of Union Hospital. It was very unusual that the vice president himself would call, so I took the phone. He informed me that the Emergency Department was swamped with patients seeking pain medications, as their physicians had been suspended. I realized my civic responsibility and agreed to take them.

Subsequently, the office was immersed in patients on very high dosages of pain medicines. Many of them were on multiple pain medications, and they had been taking them for years. They were adamant that these medications were helping them, relieving their pain, and improving their functioning. Their medical histories were complex and vague, often complicated with multiple accidents and traumas. Information related to their treatment was insufficient. We tried to get information from the previous health care provider, but the office was shut down, so no one even picked up the phone.

The patients were in the office and expecting continuity of care. As the number of prescriptions written from the office climbed, it created a red flag. A pharmacist working for Walgreen's pharmacy, while talking to a DEA agent, mentioned that she's seen a sudden increase in prescriptions coming out of Tri-State Health, which sparked an investigation. That ended up in a thrilling drama.

This book is intended for the general public, people who are concerned about what can happen if they experience a painful condition in their lifetimes. The book is also helpful for health care workers, particularly those dealing with pain. My goal is to inform the regulatory authorities that when taking such actions, they should be based on science and research rather than on their perception. The statutory proceedings regarding such matters must be diligent and ensure that due process is maintained and improve transparency and justice.

This is a true story of a physician offering help to patients left stranded when the regulatory authorities launched adverse action against health care providers who prescribed pain medications. In 1995, pain was declared as the fifth vital, necessitating health care providers to ask about pain and provide pain management that might require narcotic pain medications. The first missing link differentiating pain with other vital signs was that pain is subjective.

Second, there is no specific definition of pain; it could be discomfort, suffering, distress, unpleasantness, ache, and so many other ways described by the patients.

Third, it could have psychosocial causes, with no bodily injury that can be ascertained or central causes that cannot be isolated by routine diagnostic testing.

Fourth, there was no standardized parameter that the health care providers could reliably use to measure pain, so it was merely a patient's statement.

Fifth, no standardized pain management protocol was established; further, there were no specific standards or therapeutic dosages of narcotic pain medications, over which it could be considered abnormal, let alone overprescribing. The dose is dependent on the patient's pain response and whether the patient is narcotic naïve or tolerant. To make this more complex, earlier research indicated addiction was a rare complication of pain medicine. The result was an influx of an enormous number of pain medications. Many drug companies started advertising, as a vast narcotic market built up in the USA.

> Purdue paid certain doctors ostensibly to provide educational talks to other health care professionals and serve as consultants, but in reality to induce them to prescribe more OxyContin. Purdue paid kickbacks [and developed] contracts with certain specialty pharmacies to fill prescriptions for Purdue's opioid drugs that other pharmacies had rejected as potentially lacking medical necessity.

Purdue was convincing doctors to prescribe its product, as it was a safe and effective treatment, and even paid for a "doctor speaker program to induce those doctors to write more prescriptions of Purdue's opioid products." Drug culture flourished in the USA. At the same time, many physicians were successfully sued for undertreatment of pain. The NIDA (National Institute of Drug Abuse) reported that prescriptions for opiates escalated from around 40 million in 1991 to nearly 180 million in 2007, with the US their biggest consumer.

Regulatory authorities initiated unprecedented attacks to suspend or restrict medical licenses of health care providers who, in their views, were overprescribing pain medicines. The actions were hectic, without considering the ground realities, consequences, education, and training needed to wean patients off pain medicines gradually, as well as future strict measures before initiating any narcotic pain medicines. Their actions were merely a manifestation of power, rather than the application of any research or science. The hectic approach overlooked continuity of care for patients who were dependent on pain medications. The goal was solely to suspend doctors, who were to be made an example for others; they thought it would resolve the prevailing drug culture. But patients who were dependent on these medicines became helpless, as health care providers declined to accept any new patients with pain.

Many patients who could not find any health care providers went to the street. Some of them were involved in criminal activities, like stealing drugs, forging prescriptions, robbing pain medication from other patients, or buying the drug on the street. Many committed suicide. With increasing demand, the street drug business boomed. New drugs were introduced to the market, and some of these new drugs were highly toxic and life-threatening, amounting to an astonishingly increased incidence of fatalities.

Bushwhacked is my story, the story of a physician who agreed to accept some of these stranded patients.

The story is entirely true, and it is my rationale for telling this cautionary tale and the source of my anguish and frustration. I hope it will help to provide better care for those who need pain management.

CHAPTER 1

I n December 2011, I was in Chicago, attending a conference conducted by the International Society for Clinical Densitometry (ISCD). Joseph, my DEXA scan technician, and I had prepared to participate in this conference for a long time.

I am basically an internal medicine–trained physician, with added qualifications in pain management, addiction, sleep medicine, and medical weight management. My objective was to provide comprehensive care, so I always wanted to add credentials to benefit my patients. The DEXA scan (which measures bone density and body composition) would help me quickly determine bone density, fracture risk, and exact body fat determination. The measurement of weight and BMI (Basic Metabolic Index) are the indirect determination of body composition, specifically fat. So we bought a DEXA scan and were learning its usage. To be certified in DEXA scan reading, I went for training and took a certification examination. The visit to Chicago to attend an annual conference, where they would provide training and CME (Continuing Medication Education). Joseph accompanied me, as he intended to acquire certification in the procedure's technical part.

My goal always was to be a doctor and to serve the neediest populations, where doctors are hesitant to go. My journey to become a doctor—completing my residency to practicing medicine—was a struggle due to limited financial resources; furthermore, traveling to a foreign land to acquire higher education and training was extremely challenging. I graduated from medical college in Pakistan and dreamed to do residency in the United States. Hard work and focusing on the goal helped me to get over the hurdles I encountered. Doctors who earn their MD locally and who are US nationals are given first priority for residency training; then foreign doctors compete for the remaining residency positions. It's often many years before many foreign doctors are accepted for residency in the States.

Joseph and I also wanted to see Chicago, which is known as an alpha city (or world city) for its worldwide economic and cultural influence. As much as I enjoy the culinary offerings in my hometown, Karachi, Pakistan, Devon Avenue in Chicago is famous for Indian and Pakistani-style restaurants, with a variety of options reflecting the flavors of subcontinents. Joseph and I were excited to see Chicago and to have the opportunity to enjoy eating food that was familiar to my history, culture, and palate in the restaurants on Devon Avenue.

The conference went smoothly, and the weekend ended quickly. Our flight was scheduled to depart for Delaware on Sunday evening.

We reached the airport on time, but our flight was delayed. We checked in and went to the preboarding area. As we waited for the plane, I checked my email and noticed one from my attorney, Mr. James Kipp. I immediately opened it and saw something I could not believe. I was shocked to see the message, which included a statement that read, "The Secretary of State is issuing an order for immediate revocation or suspension to your Controlled Substance license."

I could not believe it! How could this have happened? What were the allegations? I considered this statement to be without merit and wondered if my email had been hacked. I was in shock and did not know what to do next.

My mind was flooded with thoughts. Apparently, my feelings of anxiety and confusion were clear on my face. I didn't know what to do. Joseph, sitting next to me, saw the change in my complexion and asked, "Dr. Niaz, are you OK?"

I didn't know how to express myself, but I explained, calmly and politely, "My attorney has sent me an email asking me to meet with him immediately. The Secretary of State has issued a letter to take disciplinary action on my Controlled Substance license."

"What? Why?"

I shook my head. "I do not know."

Joseph gave me a puzzled look, as if I might be hiding some facts, or perhaps he was skeptical about my not understanding the basis for the disciplinary action. "Why don't you call your attorney?" he suggested.

"It is Sunday evening. I don't think I should bother him at this time."

Joseph, however, was adamant. "You should call him."

At that moment, they announced it was time to board the plane. I knew I had extraordinarily little time to act, and if I did not, the journey would be harrowing for my peace of mind! By the time I would reach Delaware, it would be much too late to call Mr. Kipp or any other resource. I decided to call him.

To my surprise, Mr. Kipp answered the phone. After a rushed greeting, I asked him, "Did you send me an email?" I was still hopeful, even though this would be an unwelcome problem, that my email had been compromised and that the email was fraudulent.

Unfortunately, he replied, "I did. When are you coming back?"

"I'm waiting to board the plane and should be back in a few hours."

He assured me I was in good hands, and he would defend me with a "good outcome." He advised me to relax and to see him in the morning.

After that telephone conversation, I felt more at ease and was able to breathe, with more confidence that the order would be reversed. Confident in my ethical practice and standards, I felt strongly that there must have been a terrible misunderstanding or miscommunication. I told Joseph what my lawyer had to say, and he replied, "Don't worry; nothing will happen to you."

My father was a professor of accounting and wanted me to follow his profession. He grew up in Pratabgarh, Uttar Pradesh, India, and was employed by the army at the time of partition of the subcontinent into Pakistan and India. He had the option to choose between Pakistan or India, and he opted for Pakistan. He was his parents' only son, so this was a very bold decision, as this required departing from ancestors' land and a loving family, particularly parents. When he disclosed the news to his father, it was a real shock. My grandfather remained quiet, hiding his emotions, as he knew that if my father did not embark on this journey, he would lose his career.

For my father, he was emotional when he opted for Pakistan; it was excruciatingly painful. He packed up his stuff to leave several times, but he always found a reason to delay the day of departure. His mother (my grandmother) passed away when my father was very young. My grandfather never remarried, and he dedicated his life to raising his children. He also took early retirement so the children would not feel alone at home. So my father decided not to leave his father. He had already opted to join the army in Pakistan, so he would be unemployed in India, and delaying would risk losing his position in Pakistan. Finally, my grandfather assured him that he would follow my father to Pakistan, once he got settled, which provided him with enough courage to leave his home forever.

In Pakistan, he continued his education while working. Subsequently, he changed his career to teaching, as he enjoyed that, and he became a professor of accounting. The teaching position did not provide enough resources to raise the family. Therefore, he added another job, working in the morning as an Exxon Chemical accountant while teaching in the evening.

He wanted me to pursue accounting, so I entered college with a major in accounting and economics, planning to become a chartered accountant (equivalent to a certified public accounted, or CPA, in the United States). I, however, never enjoyed studying accounting and economics. My brother, a medical student, used to bring pieces of human skeleton home to study anatomy, and I found that very interesting. My father realized my aptitude and advised me to change my career to medicine.

After I graduated from medical college, I wanted to acquire higher education, preferably abroad. The goal was challenging because it required funds. I did not expect that my father could afford it, so I had to work to make my way. I had two options: either to go to England and Ireland to attain an MRCP (Member of Royal College of Physicians), or go to the USA. Initially, I opted to go to the UK and Ireland to attain an MRCP. I did part one on MRCP and needed to fulfill the requirement to sit in part two, which is the final part of acquiring a specialized degree. While in Ireland, I also sat for the VQE, the Visa Qualifying Examination for the USA.

Since I passed both examinations, I had the option to go to the USA or to continue with MRCP. I came back to Pakistan, as my son Saad Khan was born. I was delighted with the birth of my son, but my wife did not see such glee in me.

She asked, "Are you not happy with the birth of your son?"

"I am thrilled," I responded.

"You look very concerned."

"I am concerned," I admitted. "I am thinking about my career. I am not sure how long it takes to settle and to bear the expenses required to raise our son. Should I pursue my goal for higher education or find a job and get settled?"

"Discuss it with your father," she advised me.

My father advised me to continue my education. He said, "My father let me go out; therefore, I achieved so much education. Otherwise, I would be a farmer, living in a small town, so go where you are needed." He advised me to go to the USA.

It was May, and the residency positions in the USA are generally closed by February each year. It would be useless to travel now and wait for another year to apply for residency.

I went to one of my friends, Dr. Shafatullah Khan, who was also preparing to apply for residency training in the US. He advised me to go early to get a head start for the next year; plus, we could visit hospitals over there to better prepare for the interview process.

It was a callous decision for me to leave my wife with our week-old son. I was unemployed and not sure how long it would take to establish earnings. I was very skeptical, but my wife encouraged me to go, saying they would follow once I got settled.

Dr. Shafatullah Khan and I left Pakistan together and came to New York. We did not want to waste any time, so the next day, we visited various hospitals to search for any dropouts in the residency program. We managed to meet some doctors doing their residencies, and they expanded our knowledge regarding residency training. Some places in New York were risky to travel to, particularly walking on the street, wearing a suit and tie, and carrying a briefcase. We had to carry a bag with our credentials in case any hospital offered any position.

As we walked out of the subway, a policeman stopped us and advised us not to walk but to take a taxi. We were trying to save money; a taxi would be expensive.

Finally, we heard of an opening, as a candidate had dropped out, so we rushed to the hospital. The secretary informed us there were about thirty candidates scheduled to be interviewed. We still insisted that she put us on the waiting list. She was skeptical but agreed and advised us to bring our credentials, if they could find time to include us. The interview was not guaranteed. We agreed and arrived early at the hospital, hoping that this would be our first interview and would provide us some experience in interaction. Finally, I was called. The conversation went on for an unusually long time; I'd been expecting it to be a courtesy interview.

After the interview, I went home and found out about another interview in Ohio. I did not want to lose that opportunity; we had some experience now. So I decided to book a train ticket to Ohio. While in preparation for that trip, I was called by the hospital that had given me an interview; they offered me a residency position and wanted me to sign by the next day. I was speechless and surprised. The mission impossible was successfully completed.

After the harrowing experience of ending my Chicago conference with news of a potential threat to revoke one of my medical privileges, I met with my attorney the following morning. I arrived at his office around nine o'clock. I introduced myself to the receptionist, and she informed me that Mr. Kipp was expecting me and politely directed me to the conference room.

Shortly, Mr. James Kipp entered the room and greeted me warmly. We settled in our chairs, and he started the discussion. I soon realized that he was conducting an interview. His questions were diverse, reflecting all possible areas, with many questions followed by cross-questions. Some of the questions were very blunt and disconcerting to me, obviously foretelling a prosecution process.

As it was my first time in this type of prosecutorial circumstance, I was nervous. While he was questioning me, his associate worked on getting a copy of the allegations from the attorney general's office.

I heard a knock on the door. Miss Hilda, the paralegal, politely asked to enter. She had papers in her hand from the attorney general's office, and she handed them to Mr. Kipp, who glanced through them quickly. While he was reading the documents, I noticed for the first time that he seemed to be genuinely concerned. With the details of the new information provided, he stated that he would like to seek additional help from a colleague who was more familiar with medical technicalities. He asked if he could introduce me to his associate, with the assurance that his colleague, Mr. Jeff Austin, could handle the intricacies of the case much better than he.

I nodded in affirmation to his suggestion and looked for my own spiritual affirmation.

I believe in prayer, as I am fully confident that we are created by one God. Life is a test, and we will return after resurrection back to God. Often, God is referred to by different names depending on the language and religion, such as Allah in Arabic.

Being Muslim is often perceived as being unfit for modern society. Part of the problem is negative propaganda against Islam; another part of the problem is Muslim's behavior. The actual teachings of Islam emphasize selflessness and changed the objective of life from egocentricity into humanitarianism. Prophet Muhammad is referred to in the Quran in the chapter "Prophets" as, "And We have not sent you, [O Muhammad], except as a mercy to the worlds." Prophet Muhammed's (PBUH) life is a manifestation of mercy, selflessness, and sacrifices for others. He never kept even a penny overnight as savings and would not sleep until he had donated all he had to charity.

When the Christian scholars from Najran, a city in southwestern Saudi Arabia, came to the Prophet to debate Christianity versus Islam, Prophet Muhammad (PBUH) treated them as guests. He allowed them to fulfill their religious practice while staying in the mosque. In the Quran, Christians are referred to as *Nasarah*, meaning "helpers." Early Muslims strictly followed those principles, and therefore, non-Muslim and Muslims lived in harmony. Even at the time of the Ottoman Empire, churches freely functioned. You can still find a church within the residence of the Ottoman Empire, now known as Topkapi Museum; an Eastern Orthodox Church is still present in Istanbul, Turkey.

Now, Muslims are a lost nation, mainly due to a lack of scientific knowledge and interpreting Islamic jurisprudence in literal terms and a lack of application of Islamic knowledge through wisdom and science. I have always been active in mosques and other Islamic institutions. The goal was to apply actual Islamic teachings to bring humanity together and reduce or obviate Islamophobia.

When Union Hospital asked me to take some of the patients who were stranded in the emergency room because another doctor's license had been suspended, I realized my social and religious responsibilities, and therefore, I accepted as many patients as I could. They were on high dosages of pain medications, but "high dosage" is an imaginary term, as there is no "normal dosage" to compare it to. I did not realize that the licensing board was micromanaging doctors who prescribed pain medications.

Pain management is a double-edged sword. You could not satisfy a patient or the licensing board. A patient would always be upset because the doctor could not completely cover his/her pain, while the licensing board would find some way to take disciplinary action against those trying to give pain medications. Often, they used documentation to prove their case. It is often difficult, in a busy practice, to write every note like an attorney sitting in the office, rather than as a kind physician.

With Mr. Kipp's recommendation to work with his associate who was better versed in medical practice, I realized, more significantly, the potential consequence of those needing legal representation. I knew I would be comforted with prayer, and I used this time to pray for guidance and positive outcomes to a situation not expected. When I finished praying, my attorney introduced me to Mr. Jeff Austin. After a customary greeting, we settled down and resumed the discussion. Hilda, sitting beside us, placed the papers in front of Jeff.

Obviously, before accepting the case, Jeff wanted more information. He started the interrogation from the beginning—not just limited to this case but all about me and my practice, my office, and my employees, their positions, and their duties. He needed to dissect my office from every angle. He was polite in his questioning but firm.

He asked, "How do you know Mr. Kipp?"

"I had a medical student rotating with me in the office when Mr. Brady, the state investigator, came to my office with a subpoena to acquire copies of the charts. At that time, the medical student advised me to contact Mr. Kipp, inform him of the subpoena, and get his legal advice."

On August 2011, the state investigator, Mr. Brady, came to my office. He gave me a handwritten paper with a few questions on it and asked me to respond to them. He had the subpoena to get copies of my charts. I noticed that the records he was requesting were related to patients who were treated mainly by my nurse practitioner. I instructed my staff to pull the charts and make the copies. Copies of the medical records were promptly given to Mr. Brady that same day.

The first question on Mr. Brady's handwritten note concerning the practice was, "Why did the practice consistently write double prescriptions—one for cash and one for insurance?" The second question was, "Can you explain why prescriptions were written in two or sometimes three different handwritings?" He left those questions for me to answer in writing; they were to be answered to the state within a due time frame.

I explained to Jeff that I'd responded to both questions in due time, but before writing the answers, I discussed it with my office staff, including the nurse practitioner. Everyone in the office confirmed that we never wrote double prescriptions.

The nurse practitioner said, "I think what they are considering as a 'double prescription' was for some patients who had insurance restrictions on the number of pills allowed each month. When we crossed the limit, we'd have to write another prescription to cover the remaining pills. For instance, if medicine A was allowed only 120 tablets in one month, and the patient was being treated with 140 tablets per month, then the second prescription was written for the remaining twenty tablets. It is a pharmacy requirement and has nothing to do with us or calling it a double order."

I agreed with the nurse practitioner, but I called a pharmacy to discuss how to write prescriptions for medications that were not entirely covered by patients' insurance. The pharmacy informed me that the only way to fill the remaining dosage was to write another prescription for the remaining quantity.

The second question was related to handwritten prescriptions. I answered that prescriptions were written by hand. Since this was a very time-consuming procedure, we allowed one designated person to write prescriptions to save time. The provider checked and signed the prescription. Sometimes, a pharmacy did not carry the medication, and a patient had to bring the prescription back to the office, as the name of the pharmacy was also endorsed on the prescription. Then, we'd have to change the name of the pharmacy, which might appear as a third handwriting. The pharmacy never showed any dissatisfaction with this procedure. There was no requirement that the provider must write prescriptions in one handwriting.

Jeff then wanted to know what happened after that. "Did the state or the licensing board discuss these issues after you submitted your response?"

"No, they never contacted me. I assumed the inquiry was over."

After a thorough interrogation, Jeff assured me that he would take my case, and he was confident he could defend me against the allegations.

At this point in our discussion, Mr. Kipp said that the secretary of state was sending a suspension order on my controlled substance license, and he wanted to confirm whether I had received any allegations. I said no.

Mr. Kipp was in contact with the secretary of state's office and informed them that I had never received any allegations. The state then proceeded to serve the charges.

My attorney received the allegations via fax and handed them over to me. They were written in very technical language, with no names of the patients included in the documentation of what they were alleging were overprescribed medications in prescriptions. At least now, the allegations had been revealed.

I was shocked and felt helpless; it was an arrogant use of power. I could not cry or shout, as I needed to be strong and seek help from Almighty to defend my dignity and honor. The immediate thought that constantly knocked in my mind was, *Why did they never bother to discuss this with me, rather than wanting an answer in court? What were they trying to achieve?* There must be some missing link, and I could see on Mr. Kipp's face that he was also genuinely concerned. After I'd provided care to such an underserved population, I expected that the regulating authorities would appreciate rather punish me.

How this investigation originated was an enigma to me.

CHAPTER 2

The allegations I was about to face were based on the charts that Mr. Brady had demanded by subpoena back in August. The filed complaints were related to overprescription. According to these complaints, I wrote prescriptions for more than 57,000 tablets/capsules of controlled substances, including 42,000 tablets of oxycodone, within a period of six months. They mentioned four patients, who were labeled as A, B, C, and D. No indication was given as to who these patients were. The allegation referred to an office in Wilmington, where my nurse practitioner was charged with writing prescriptions for an excessive amount of medication, but I did not have an office in Wilmington. They also alleged that during those six months, my nurse practitioner wrote prescriptions for 89,000 tablets of oxycodone. Also, it was alleged that I overprescribed controlled substances to patients in amounts that exceeded safe therapeutic levels without conducting proper medical examinations, without creating and maintaining proper records or logs, without ordering tests, without requesting medical records, without contacting patients' primary care or other treating physicians, without obtaining patients' informed consent, without establishing any legitimate medical basis or need for medication, without evaluating patients' pain and determining if prescribed medications were effective, and without taking reasonable and necessary precautions to prevent illegal diversion of controlled substances. Without referring patients, they were prescribed controlled substances to another physician, therapist, counselor, or other professional, including but not limited to pain specialists or addiction counselors, to evaluate and/or treat medical, psychological, and/or addiction conditions or problems.

We needed to identify patients A, B, C, and D. For us, it was guesswork. Allegations did not accompany a key to decode the names of these patients.

As I reviewed the allegations, it became clear to me that the state had misstated "facts." For patient A, the allegations stipulated 280 tablets of alprazolam were prescribed in one prescription to a patient who was taking buprenorphine. This combination could be fatal. Furthermore, it was alleged that I prescribed fentanyl patches to the same patient. In patients B, C, and D, the allegations were related to giving medicine indiscreetly, thus manifesting a "pill mill."

The opioid epidemic has a long history of evolution, involving a multitude of factors. In the early 1900s, there was increasing usage of street heroin. Therefore, the Harrison Narcotic Control Act of 1914, passed in response to the sudden emergence of street heroin abuse and iatrogenic (given by prescribers) morphine dependence, influenced both physicians and patients alike to avoid opiates. The courts interpreted this to mean that physicians could prescribe narcotics to patients in the course of standard treatment but not for the "treatment of addiction." Opium became the first illegal drug with the passage of the Harrison Act.

In the early nineteenth century, patients requiring narcotics were often labeled as *maligning*. A term used in contemporary literature was "opiophobia," which implied fear or resistance to prescribing pain medication. This fear persisted into the latter half of the twentieth century. This caused the undertreatment of pain sufferers in those who needed pain medications. Subsequently, in the late 1900s, there was a sudden emphasis on writing prescriptions for pain medications, as the literature indicated that people with pain were suffering, despite effective pain medications. Addiction was considered a rare complication of narcotic drugs.

For example, Morgan in 1985 and Zenz and Willweber-Strumpf in 1992 both describe a state of under-reliance on opioid analgesics and resultant undertreatment of pain in Europe and North America (JP Morgan, "American opiophobia: customary underutilization of opioid analgesics," *Adv Alcohol Sust Abuse,* 1985; and M. Zenz and A. Willweber-Strumpf, "Opiophobia and Cancer pain in Europe," *Lancet,* 1993). During this period, you could find several articles that focused on the awareness of pain undertreatment.

Max described "therapeutic use of opiate analgesics rarely results in addiction" (MB Max, "Improving outcomes of analgesic treatment: is education enough?" *Ann Intern. Med,* 1990). Doctors were encouraged to take pain seriously and increase writing pain medications, as the literature indicated that almost 70 percent of the people with pain were undertreated.

Alongside this opioid evolution, the American Pain Society launched their influential "pain as the fifth vital sign" campaign in 1995, with the intent to encourage proper, standardized evaluation and treatment of pain symptoms (JN Campbell, APS 1995 presidential address, Pain Forum, 1996). Vital signs reflect essential body functions, including heartbeat, breathing rate, temperature, and blood pressure.

Some doctors were successfully sued for undertreating pain, such as *Bergman v. Eden.* In that case, tried in 2001, jurors awarded $1.5 million to the family of William Bergman. Mr. Bergman's children alleged that during their late father's hospital stay, his physician, Wing Chin, prescribed only Demerol as needed, even though Mr. Bergman registered pain levels of 7–10 on a 1–10 scale. Pain scale is subjective, as a patient indicates the level of pain that he/she is feeling. In private practice, most patients who are prescribed pain medication generally indicate 7–10 on a pain scale of 1–10; still, the regulatory authorities can allege overprescription and could successfully win the case.

Providers were persuaded to write pain medication as demanded by the patient. Because pain was declared as the fifth vital sign, it was obligatory to address pain management, much like the other vital signs—blood pressure, pulse, temperature, and respiration. The missing link was that the first four vital signs were objective; a physician could measure and confirm these signs before prescribing medications, while pain was subjective, merely a patient's statement. In order to measure pain severity, different pain scales were developed. The usual standard medical pain scale was a numeric rating scale that ranged from 1 to 10, on which 0 implies no pain, 1–3 means mild pain, 4–6 means moderate pain, and 7–10 means severe pain. As we know, people's tolerance to pain varies. One person may state his pain is 9, but for another, it could be 4. Further confusing and complex is the determination of how much pain medication is needed for any specific pain level.

This was troublesome for doctors, as patients who were received from other practices had been on pain medication for an extended period with severe tolerance. So if a patient on a high dose of pain medication showed a pain diary that indicated the patient's pain was 8–10 after taking medications, and the doctor wanted to reduce medications, the patient would be extremely difficult and often argumentative.

It was challenging to manage, as there is no specific definition or description of pain. People define pain differently—suffering, ache, pang, throb, twinge, stitch, shoot. Further, there may be no identifiable bodily pathology required to suffer from pain. It becomes more cumbersome when dealing with patients with coexisting psychiatric disorders. Not only do they describe pain in their own way, but they also feel better when prescribed narcotic pain medications. In their minds, this confirms that they have pain, as their pain is significantly reduced by pain medications. They are also at risk of committing suicide if a physician refuses to manage their pain. Suicide is common among people suffering from pain.

One patient took a large dose of pain medications; we accepted him to provide continuity of care from another doctor at the request of Union Hospital. I tried to persuade him to reduce his pain medication and rely on non-narcotic treatment. His argument was that he had tried, and nothing worked, except his current regimen. I became adamant about mitigating his pain medications. On the next visit, he looked explosive. I asked him how he was doing.

He responded, "Miserably." Before I could proceed with further questioning, he asked, "Why did you try to cut my medications?"

I tried to explain the side effects of these medications.

He became furious and asked me why the other doctors had prescribed these pain medications all these years. "Doc, this was the only thing left in my life that helped me keep going, but you want to cut them off. Doc! You are lucky, as I came with a gun but have decided not to shoot you."

I realized the gravity of the situation and felt I had to continue his pain medications, but I advised him to find another doctor for his pain medications. Adverse actions by the regulatory authorities against doctors who prescribe pain medications have been a threat to doctors to stop writing prescriptions for pain medications.

Patients are often forced to buy street drugs. Therefore, there was an increase in the usage of street drugs, particularly after 2010. This is well documented in all epidemiological surveys—as prescription writing decreased, use of street drugs proportionately went up. Street drugs are extremely dangerous and can even be fatal, like acetyl fentanyl, acrylfentanyl, 3-methy fentanyl ("China White"), butyrfentanyl, U-47700, and carfentanil, which have been reported to be fifteen to ten thousand times more potent than morphine. They are sold on the street in almost every city and town of the United States. More alarming is that they are very economical and are easily available. Drug dealers have put these drugs on sale as they noticed an increase in demand and market. Street drugs also have adulterants, which are added to increase the bulk and to potentiate the drug's effects. A common example is levamisole, which causes *agranulocytosis*, destruction of white cells that provide immunity to fight against infection and causes vasculitis, damaging the blood vessels, resulting in a limited capacity to carry blood to the tissues.

New drugs were introduced to the market, like crystal meth, which is extremely dangerous and potent. Before that, people were only aware of amphetamine and cocaine as stimulant drugs. Then, clandestine labs realized the increasing need and synthesized crystal meth (methylamphetamine— street name "ice") and "bath salts," a synthetic cathinone synthesized in the lab that has a similar effect to cocaine and amphetamine. More such compounds have flooded the street market.

With the list of specific and alleged overprescription to four individual patients, my immediate reaction stemmed from the inaccuracy of what I read. *Something must be wrong!* I thought. *I am a conservative prescriber, and it is not possible that anyone from my office could have written these prescriptions.* I feared unusual or suspect behavior. Had someone stolen my prescription pads? Were prescriptions written in my name and/or in the name of my nurse practitioner? I did not have an office in Wilmington. How could they allege that I had an office there?

We did not have the names of patients A, B, C, and D, and time was running out before the requested deadline. At that time, the goal was to get more time to answer those allegations. Jeff wanted to respond immediately to the allegations because it might provide a chance to place a hold on the suspension order. The tension was mounting with every passing hour. It was an exceptionally long meeting. We had to figure out the names of these patients. I asked to go to my office to meet with my office staff and try to figure out who these patients were—we had to identify those patients that day.

I drove faster than usual to get back to my office so that my staff and I could work on identifying those four patients. It was like solving a puzzle. The staff was waiting for me with a faxed copy of the allegations that I had sent to them. Slowly, we figured out who the four patients were from the descriptions given in the allegations and a thorough review of patient files. We pulled their charts, and in doing so, we found that the allegations were full of errors and inaccuracies. Sadly, the regulatory authority threatened me with a very unethical approach!

In one prescription, the state had alleged that I prescribed 280 tablets of Xanax to a patient; the number was actually twenty-eight. We also called the pharmacy to verify the amount of medication that was dispensed. The pharmacy said that the patient received only twenty-eight tablets. It was beyond my understanding where the state got their allegation that the patient received 280 tablets.

This particular patient was a schoolteacher who had detoxified from heroin usage. After detoxification, her pulse remained elevated, and her ECG showed tachycardia, which continued over twenty-four hours. Other withdrawal symptoms were well controlled; therefore, Xanax was added to help in case of anxiety. After her pulse reduced, she was referred to a cardiologist, who agreed with the plan and added a beta-blocker. The state highlighted this issue, most likely linked to the incidental report mentioned in the *Physicians' Desk Reference* (PDR), where a few patients with addiction simultaneously injected the combination of buprenorphine and benzodiazepine intravenously and died.

It is not a contraindication to prescribe both drugs together; that drug combination can be used carefully. In fact, millions of patients in America have been prescribed that combination as a remedy for anxiety and panic symptoms, as these ailments often coexist with addiction. The PDR issued a precaution to the treating provider, but it is not absolutely contraindicated. Also, the PDR does not dictate the standard of care but does give helpful information to a treating physician.

Again, in the case of patient A, precautions were applied, documented, and later discontinued. She responded well to the treatment and was able to continue her teaching responsibilities. Unfortunately, a few months later, she was involved in a motor vehicle accident. While in the hospital, her buprenorphine/naloxone medication was halted, and she was placed on a narcotic pain medication, which required continuation on the fentanyl patch and dilaudid. At no point in her treatment was she prescribed any buprenorphine/naloxone together with any other narcotics. The state alleged that she received both drug treatments. She did well with her post-accident surgery and was placed back on suboxone after her injury improved, but her narcotic pain medications were discontinued.

Regarding patients B, C, and D, there were pieces of evidence of multiple gross errors by the state. For patient B, the state alleged that medications were overprescribed, and he had been accepted by another medical office that had closed unexpectedly. That office had closed because the physician who owned the practice had lost his license. As a result, patients were pouring into Union Hospital's Emergency Department. At that time, Union Hospital's vice president asked me to accept some of those stranded patients to provide continuity of care and to clear out the emergency demand. It would have been detrimental to both the hospital and the patients if I had refused the request. I performed my civic responsibility and accepted the patients that I could. Those patients were clearly on high dosages of pain medications. My goal was to reduce their medications slowly and not harm them.

To investigate appropriately, the state had to review each patient, the whole course of treatment, and extenuating circumstances related to each case and not merely the number of medicines prescribed. Furthermore, the state also overreported the number of drugs prescribed to patient B. Again,

I was significantly concerned with the inaccuracies of their reporting because of a perception of a "pill mill" environment.

Patient C also came from another practice and was followed by the nurse practitioner. Subsequently, the nurse practitioner referred the patient to me. I saw him one time but had to discharge him for noncompliance.

Patient D was a male patient with hepatitis C, which was complicated by severe back pain and critical arthritis, confirmed by MRI scanning, and therefore was on pain medications. I was volunteering a free service to the Brandywine Rehabilitation Center to provide free hepatitis C treatment, as patients in their care belong to an underserved population. Due to a desire to continue treatment for hepatitis, patient C started following me in my office. The state overstated his medications too. This patient did not begin his narcotic pain medications from my office. Instead, he came with a high dosage that I later reduced.

This was another terrible error on the part of the state. The error was in not finding out who had started pain medication and why and whether or not the patient was compliant with the medication. Was there a diversion involved? They should have looked at the course of treatment with us. What happened with the patient? Did we reduce the medications or increase them? There should have been a communication where they expressed their concerns, but apparently, they just wanted to win the case. They only focused on the number of pills prescribed, and even that was tabulated grossly wrong, as there was another patient with the same name but a different date of birth. The state failed to identify these individuals as two separate patients, so they combined the prescriptions of these two patients and projected it as given to one patient. Obviously, it looked excessive.

I called the pharmacy to check if there were errors in dispensing medications from my office, but found none. Again, this was an overinflated projection. The pharmacy profile clearly stated the different birth dates, which any competent investigator should have differentiated quickly and easily.

Accepting new patients with complex medical issues was not easy. The pain was the dominating symptom but was complicated by multiple medical problems. We had to add staff and realized the changing culture of the office. Safety was one concern; compliance was the second concern. How we could force patients to be compliant? We often relied on urine toxicology, but that is not a foolproof system.

Another problem was that if the patient refused to reduce pain medications and ultimately was discharged, he or she had a very high risk of suicide, and the patient might not find another provider. One young woman had three children but was not compliant with the medication. Her urine toxicology came positive with cocaine a couple of times, so I decided to discharge the patient from the practice. After a few days, her family informed me that she had died due to a drug overdose, probably from highly toxic street drugs.

We caught many patients doing adulteration in prescriptions. We added measures to prevent diversion, including introducing a raised seal. This ensured that the prescriptions were written from the office and that prescription pads were not stolen or forge printed. Also, we secured the quantity by writing it numerically and alphabetically.

Controlled medications, mainly Schedule II, should copy the prescription kept in the chart and have a pharmacy name written on it. Each patient had to sign a pain agreement, which was a combination of promises, expectations, and education regarding the side effect of these medications.

These patients were mainly on Medicaid, with limited access to medications and consultations. Often, advanced diagnostic workups required prior authorization, which was challenging and needed to go through a tedious process—and often was denied. Choice of medications was limited. Mainly short-acting narcotic drugs were in their listed formulary, and almost all of the long-acting medications required prior authorizations and were not easy to get.

We also needed staff who were experienced in dealing with pain management. Often, the office had to play a police role and watch patient behavior. Were they taking anything with them to the restroom? Was the urine submitted genuine and not adulterated? The problem was even more complicated with women. Often, they came with their children and took them to the restroom with them. We had a strict policy of not taking anything, including children, into the toilet. They would argue, asking where they could leave their children. They were hesitant to leave their children outside. We introduced a body-search policy, where a patient would undergo a complete body search to ensure that he or she could not take any hidden outside urine inside; this was to prevent adulteration.

They used so many genius tricks to hide urine inside their bodies that I wondered if they could have bested Einstein if they had used their intelligence in the right direction. Girls were almost impossible to check fully, as they could hide urine in the vagina. We couldn't do a pelvic examination of each woman before prescribing pain medications each time.

Every day, we had new discoveries of how to break the system. Another technique they used was one patient putting urine in a trash can, and the person following would take it from the trash can and inside the restroom. Checking the trash can after each person came out of the toilet also was impossible. Checking the temperature of urine as soon as we received the sample became mandatory. Despite acting as police, the system looked fragile, but our main goal was patient safety and a proper standard of care.

CHAPTER 3

We all learn by our mistakes or haste. I fully expected, with the numerous errors in the allegations, that the state would clearly recognize there was no avarice or neglect involved in our practice. Our first goal was to put a hold on any suspension order by the secretary of state. Therefore, we wanted to draft a letter quickly, stating these errors and responding to all allegations adequately within the next two weeks.

I immediately drafted a document to my attorney, highlighting the numerous errors. Jeff asked Mr. Kipp to follow this document with a quick response to the secretary of the state. By the next day, Mr. Kipp wrote a comprehensive letter to the secretary of state that was both conservative and humble. In his letter, dated December 7, 2011, he briefly described errors made by the state and requested more time for a complete response. He wrote:

> Because time is of the essence since State is petitioning for immediate revocation or suspension of Dr. Niaz's controlled substance registration, this letter addresses only that issue and is not intended as a complete response to the Complaints. My client and I will make every effort to file a complete response with detailed factual information to each allegation, within the next two weeks.

This letter was immediately hand-delivered to the Office of the Secretary of State.

After that, I hoped that the secretary would give us one or two more weeks to answer those allegations. It seemed clear to us that the state investigators were trying to find ways to prove their case, rather than a continued evaluation of factual data and the truth.

The question in my mind was, *Why is the investigator one-sided?* Legally, investigators should be neutral and should look for the facts, not try to prove what the state had deduced, based on their own chart review. They were required to give us a chance to respond to any complaint before initiating any adverse action. Instead, they approached the secretary of state to revoke and/or suspend my controlled substance registration. Obviously, these actions generally were justified by stating they were "in the interest of the public."

The *News Journal* was writing articles over the past many weeks before the state action regarding drug epidemics. The focus was to highlight iatrogenic drug prescriptions as the primary source of the street drug market. They projected how profitable this business was, as they wrote this was "the only commodity which is many folds cheaper at the pharmacy than at the street, decorating a stage to win the case." The aim was to shift public opinion to believe that the problem of drugs on the street was mainly due to physicians and that punishing doctors would solve the problem of the drugs epidemic in the country. Also, the people who sat in deliberation would be influenced by such news.

The government was looking for ways to stop the drug epidemic. Politicians could take adverse action against some physicians and make an example of them in the community to scare other physicians away from prescribing pain medications. It was pivotal for politicians to attest to cavalier leadership and to make an elite leader run as a presidential candidate. They needed an easy target or a sacrificial lamb, so the selection fell on two physicians—one was Afro American, and the other was Asian American.

Prejudice and discrimination are not new. History is loaded with such behavior—the concept that I am better than you. A markedly overweight woman who worked in my office indicated that she had always been a victim of discrimination.

I said, "You are white. Why do people discriminate against you?"

"My weight is the reason for discrimination," she said.

When God gives someone a blessing, he or she should be thankful; unfortunately, some people become arrogant.

I was expecting a favorable answer from the secretary of state. The next day, I called my attorney to inquire about it. He replied, "No answer!" I was anxious yet confident, knowing that I never overprescribed any pain medication. Still, I was fearful of how the investigation was unfolding and being conducted. Many questions erupted in my mind. Were they planning to frame me? They might need a harsh punishment for a physician to convey a message to all those prescribing pain medications. In other words, was I to be a sacrificial lamb?

The governor established a task force to focus on drug trafficking, sales, and other illegal drug-related activities. Their job was to search for activities linked to drug abuse. They could provide valuable information to physicians regarding drug diversion, and such patients should be discharged from the practice. The physicians and providers were never in the loop and were considered as part of the problem. Therefore, the task force was being used to investigate physicians, instead stop drug diversion, like drug dealers.

Medical health providers have the right to know if any of their patients are selling or diverting drugs or are involved in any such activities. Providers are on the front line, and if they are not supplied with enough resources, they then have to depend on what is presented within the office. The decision is often based on a patient's information, and when health providers are not sure, providers will err on the side of the patient's safety. If a patient has been on pain medication for an extended period, sudden denial of the medication could be catastrophic.

I have no problem prescribing pain medication to someone who is taking the medication religiously, and it's helping the patient to function better and is easing suffering, but I would not allow drug abuse or diversion. In this context, the task force would help doctors by providing reliable information. Unfortunately, the task force's goal is to find fault in order to investigate physicians, even though members of the task force are often laymen who never worked in a medical field and didn't have prior medical training. They didn't even know how to count the patient's actual drug intake or understand why it was prescribed or how to use the pharmacy profile.

On December 8, 2011, I took a day off to visit my children who were studying in New York and New Jersey. While I was there, my cell phone rang. The call was from one of my office staff, who indicated that the investigator, Mr. Brady, was there, accompanied by another person.

"What did they say?" I asked.

"They just asked about you. I said you'd be available tomorrow, and they said they'd return then." My staff was frightened and wondered if they would have jobs the next day. They then looked on the licensing board's webpage for any clues. They were astonished by what they saw—the webpage indicated that my controlled substance license had been suspended.

When they told me, I was speechless! Right away, I called my attorney to see if he had heard from the secretary of state. He had not. Now that the licensing board had posted a suspension of my license, the intentions of the state were quite clear. It was a traumatic, outrageous lie against a physician on a public platform.

I find it difficult to find words to express my feelings. I know people of color have to face discrimination at every stage of their lives, but I was expecting a justifiable approach from a public organization. Their message, however, was clear and loud—they needed a sacrificial lamb or scapegoat, and who would be a better choice than a colored foreign Muslim?

The following day, I left New Jersey early to get to my office by 9:00 a.m. It was an incredibly stressful drive. I thought that Mr. Brady would be there with a suspension order. On the two-hour drive from New Jersey to Delaware, I had to stop a couple of times to catch my breath.

I felt overwhelmed by fear and anxiety. When I arrived at my office, my staff was anxiously waiting. Before I could take off my overcoat, they gathered in my office, offering their opinions and their thoughts on the matter.

Azahar (known as AZ), a staff member, said, "Today, the licensing board's website shows that your controlled substance license is active. Yesterday, it was inactive."

I could see the state was keen to act. Yesterday, they had suspended my controlled substance registration before coming to my office, but because they had not been able to meet with me, to be legally correct they had to show my license as active until they handed over the allegations. Today, they probably would serve and suspend me at the same time. Another possibility was a reversal or significant change in their actions because the secretary of state had read the letter written by my attorney.

I had patients scheduled for that day and didn't know what to do. Should I see my patients or wait until the investigator came to my office to clarify the situation? Without a controlled substance registration, I would be extremely limited in prescribing medications. I decided to wait for the investigator to clarify the status of my license.

In the midst of the discussion with staff, two cars pulled into my driveway. Mr. Brady, the investigator for the state, was in one of the vehicles, and a man I later learned was a DEA agent was in the other. They entered the office and showed their identification.

We moved to a patient room and closed the door. Mr. Brady indicated that he was there to serve me with the allegations. He presented the same papers that my attorney had showed me in his office a few days earlier. I asked Mr. Brady to allow me a few days to respond, and I assured him that my response would be exceptionally satisfactory. I started showing him errors in the allegations to convince him to give me some time.

He listened very attentively to the details, often nodding, but he could not change the plans. "You have to come to the hearing to explain these details," he said. "I will come back on Monday to give you a suspension letter from the secretary of state."

After I finished conversing with Mr. Brady, the man from the DEA put a paper in front of me. By signing this document, I would be stating that I had voluntarily given up my DEA license. A controlled substance registration is issued by the state, while the DEA license is issued by the federal government. Both licenses are required to prescribe controlled medications for medicinal use. In a demanding tone, he ordered me to sign the document. Technically, once the secretary of state had issued the suspension on my controlled substance registration, I could not prescribe controlled medications. I looked at the document and thought, *Why would I sign?*

There was no allegation from the DEA, and my signing would imply that I voluntarily accepted the claims from the state and gave up my DEA license as well. Any citizen of the United States of America has a fundamental right to discuss legal matters with an attorney before making a decision, so I tried to exercise that right. I told him, "I need to discuss signing this document with my attorney."

He then violently threatened me, shouting, "Dr. Niaz, you don't need to discuss anything! If you don't sign, I will bring a criminal case against you by this evening!"

This was a serious threat by someone representing the DEA in an official capacity.

Politely, I continued talking, hoping to convince him to allow me to at least inform my attorney. There was no change in his behavior. He expected my signature without any debate. He was firm that my attorney would poorly advise me.

I realized that the situation was getting out of control as he began threatening my staff, shouting that he would tear down the whole office. I always had the impression that the DEA was a professional organization, run by rules and regulations, but what I was witnessing was completely opposite of that.

Finally, I promised to sign, even if my attorney advised me not to sign. After much back-and-forth arguing, he seemed reassured that I would sign the document and that the purpose of my calling my attorney was just for information. I was finally granted permission to call my attorney. Jeff quickly understood the situation by my tone; he did not stop me, as he realized it was useless to argue with the DEA officer. One reprieve I was shown was my being allowed to continue patient care for another day. Another reprieve was my being allowed to continue practicing in Maryland because the DEA restriction was limited to Delaware. Before leaving the office, he announced that the suspension order would be effective on Monday.

After signing the papers, I continued my conversation with Mr. Brady, trying to dismiss the allegations or at least hoping he would grant me more time to file an answer to the allegations. I expected more empathy. Mr. Brady advised me to come to the hearing in a few weeks to answer the charges.

What would I say to patients who needed continuous care? Should I refer them elsewhere? Where would they go? I felt as though my patients would be stranded because I did not know what type of arrangements I could make. I was on my own regarding these patients, with no provider to whom I could refer them.

As he left the office, Mr. Brady informed me that he would be back on Monday to bring the suspension order from the secretary of state. Meanwhile, I realized there had been no point in our discussion because the only way to fix this was to make my case at the hearing. In the meantime, my controlled substance registration and DEA would remain suspended.

On Saturday, December 10, 2011, the *News Journal* placed the story on the front page with the headline, "State Officials Suspend Three in Probe."

> "Besides prescribing the drugs in unsafe doses, all three ignored evidence that patients were abusing or diverting drugs to illegal uses," State officials said. "Delaware law allows the state to take such action when officials determine that the prescriber is an 'imminent danger' to the public. ... It is critically important that we prevent these three individuals from continuing to pose a significant risk to the public by removing their ability to prescribe controlled substances," Bullock said. "There are some ongoing severe investigations, as well as cases outlined in these complaints, the allegation were severe and possible leading to criminal panishment ," Bullock said.

Three providers were mentioned in the news report; the first two were my nurse practitioner and me. Who was the third one whose license was suspended? I learned he was an African American doctor, practicing in Dover, Delaware.

The state had already convicted me by suspending my license without allowing me a response. The news spread like wildfire! The combination of the state concluding and announcing their findings and the voluntary surrender of DEA licenses—mine and my nurse practitioner's—made the presumption of guilt inevitable. Despite it all, I was graciously supported by a few friends—Dr. Ali Khan, Br. Bilal BMA, and Dr. Naveed Baqir came to my home to ask what had happened. They offered their prayers, support, and help from elected officials, but I knew this was a legal battle that I had to fight personally at the state hearing.

The negative publicity in the news made it impossible to have a fair hearing. Insurance companies and hospitals withdrew their privileges. My malpractice insurance company notified me it was terminating my coverage at the end of the week and sent me an invoice to pay $27,000 to have tail coverage. Things seemed to be going from bad to worse. Furthermore, if I lost my malpractice insurance, I would not be able to continue my medical practice in Maryland. It was a nightmare! I used to think the worst thing that could happen to anyone was death, but what I was experiencing was far more troubling and painful.

That following week, I called the Medical Society of Delaware to see if they could help me extend my malpractice insurance until the hearing, which was scheduled for January 25, 2012. I explained these were allegations, not a conviction, and emphasized the need to continue my malpractice coverage. They agreed to intervene on my behalf to get an extension of my malpractice insurance at least until the hearing.

On Monday, December 12, 2011, Mr. Brady came back to my office. This time, he was there to serve me with the temporary suspension on my controlled substance registration as ordered by the secretary of state. The order stated that "findings based on the allegations contained within the State's complaint, there existed an imminent danger to the public health or safety warranting such action." Even though the order was limited to the state of Delaware, it affected me globally. The reach of the internet and electronic sources left no room for my privacy. It was going to be an uphill battle, even to practice in Maryland. The newspapers in Cecil County, Maryland—the *Cecil Whig* and the *Newark Post*—followed the news printed by the *News Journal*. Friends began keeping their distance from me, and social and religious organizations started asking me to voluntarily resign. My relatives were keeping distant and silent and did not want to associate with me, probably fearful I might ask them for financial support. My immediate family members—my wife and children—did not wish to receive any phone calls or see anyone. My mother and wife were in constant prayer, often with tears overflowing from their eyes.

Pharmacies in Maryland stopped filling my prescriptions. Rumors were spreading like wildfire. It was merely a formality to go to the hearing in January in Delaware, to be followed by a reciprocal action by the Maryland licensing board. To clarify my position, I called the Maryland licensing board and informed them of my current status, which they already knew, but they did not provide any specific advice. My Maryland license was still active, and there was no reason for pharmacies to deny my prescriptions. Elkton Friendly Pharmacy, however, which was a pharmacy near my office, was so agitated to see my prescriptions that not only did they refuse to fill the prescriptions, but they also sent a copy of the newspaper article to the medical licensing board with the prescription. It was a challenge to find a pharmacy willing to fill my prescriptions, despite my written letter to them, stating that both my Maryland license and DEA license were active and unrestricted. Patients needed continuity of care, and without prescriptions filled, medical care was meaningless.

Some pharmacies approached the pharmacy board to issue an order to stop filling prescriptions written by my office. The pharmacy board called a general board meeting in the form of hearing the issue and to decide what line of action should be taken. This was just more chaos. I thought of attending their hearing to defend my case, but due to time constraints and my wanting to be fully prepared to go to the hearing in Delaware, I made the choice to leave it to them to make any decision. I did not hear of any adverse action from them.

In the meantime, my staff suggested I write a brief summary of the case and send it to all the pharmacies in the area so that they could better understand that this office was not a "pill mill," as portrayed in the media. I wrote what they asked, explaining the misunderstanding concerning what appeared to be excessive overprescription of pain medication. After receiving the letter, a few pharmacists agreed to fill my prescriptions.

In the letter, I explained the whole situation and hoped they would continue filling the prescription, as the matter needed to be vetted through a hearing, and I was confident of winning the case. The most important point I mentioned was the continuity of patient care—interruption could have dangerous outcomes.

Many Delaware patients were desperately trying to find another medical provider, and many of them went to hospital emergency rooms (ERs). Without question, many of them probably went to street corners to score their pain medications. I still remember one woman who worked for the police department. I got that patient from Dr. Donohue, who had passed away. She had rheumatoid arthritis and was on a high dosage of pain medications, and she developed incredibly significant tolerance. Anyone reviewing her medications might think that she was overprescribed, but in reality, that dosage was keeping her functional and able to work. She was looking for another doctor but could not find one. After a month or so, I got the news that she had died. I did not know the cause of her death, but certainly stopping her medications played a key role; whether she committed suicide was not apparent but remained a possibility.

Overprescription is a vague term with different meanings to different people. Overprescription or overmedication alludes to unnecessary or excessive medicines prescribed. In medical conditions, there is no specific dosage of narcotic pain medications. An appropriate dose is an effective dose, while considering tolerance, side effects, functional status, comorbid conditions, ceiling effects, and, of course, insurance coverage. Neither the *Physicians' Desk Reference* nor the CDC gives any specific dosage over which it is considered overdosage. There is no ceiling effect, which implies no further impact on pain above a particular dosage. Therefore, a provider may need to titrate dosage. For example, a patient who may need 30 mg of morphine today may require 200 mg of morphine after a few years. A patient who has developed tolerance may need a prescription that is manyfold higher. Can an investigator or a prosecutor who looks at the number of pills prescribed say for sure, without seeing the patient, that the drug was overprescribed? No.

A physician determines the correct dose to titrate the minimum effective dose. In a drug-naïve patient, this may be small, but the patient dose could be extremely high in a patient who has drug tolerance. To prove overprescribing requires the prosecutive authority to confirm the wrong outcome to a patient or a detriment in functioning, prominent side effects, and compromising other comorbid conditions. If the prosecutor based the case on diversion, then there should be some evidence that proves diversion and that such pieces of evidence were available to the physician at the time of prescribing medications. Therefore, without bringing proper proof—either by directly examining a patient or at least bring a document of harmful consequences on a patient—it is a baseless allegation. They humiliate a physician in public to create fear and deterrence.

Preparation for the hearing was not easy because there was no discovery. Legally, the prosecutor should send the findings of the expert who reviewed the chart to the doctor being investigated. Here, this was an open-ended prosecution. Whatever they could think, they could ask, and we had to defend in that moment. It involved thoroughly reviewing all related charts, digging through every description, and determining if diagnosis and documentation justified the dosage. I was focused on how the prosecutor would manipulate the notes and/or medication dosages to link them to the allegations.

With the invention of electronic medical records (EMRs), charts became extremely voluminous. Details might be repeated over several encounters. Many EMRs had a default setting that added standard information in the examination and "review of systems." Information from other providers, laboratory workups, x-rays, diagnostic studies, consultations notes, pharmacy and other miscellaneous papers needed to be identified and reviewed. It was tedious preparing for the hearing but vital to be able to answers any possible questions. Our limited preparation time forced us to work exhaustive hours while spending the day seeing patients in the Maryland office.

CHAPTER 4

O n the day of the hearing, I arrived at the courtroom early. Jeff, my attorney, and Hilda, a paralegal, were already there and were waiting for me. The location for the hearing was a house that looked like an isolated farmhouse or a jail in a rural area, instead of a courtroom. It probably was an old jail covered with well-demarcated walls so a person could not run away. Security appeared to be very tough. The television and news media were there, with a live telecast of the entire event.

The prosecuting authority had invited multiple organizations— Medicaid, Medicare, and the task force from nearby states were identified—to further investigate other possible criminality. There were also numerous "white-collars," sharply dressed men, dangerous-looking observers, probably undercover detectives. The prosecution was confident the case was straightforward and merely a formality. The battleground was well set, and forces were placed in strategic positions. Stakes were high on both sides. A victory for the prosecution would commence a fatal attack on doctors who dared to prescribe pain medications. Representatives from the state, in a *News Journal* interview, had already suggested criminal links, which were under consideration. For the defense, it was a matter of dignity and a fight for patients who deserved to have pain medications to reduce suffering; otherwise, the only medication a doctor could write would be for Tylenol or ibuprofen. The other fear was injustice, as the setup looked ominous, overwhelming, and hopeless.

Jeff looked overly concerned, but being a professional, he kept his composure while also keeping me relaxed.

Attorneys are expensive. Because I'd paid malpractice insurance over many years, I was confident that insurance would cover my attorney's fees. I had eye-opening and traumatic news when Jeff informed me that the malpractice insurance had decline to cover the cost.

When insurance companies sell the policy, they advertise buying a standard claims-made insurance policy that covers alleged medical errors. But now that there were alleged medical errors, they found a way out by stating that the errors alleged by the regulatory authority were excluded from the coverage. It was simply a loophole in the law. Any doctor buying a medical policy would not think that way. Error is error. If the insurance says they cover the error, then they cannot later say, "Well, this error is alleged by so-and-so, so your malpractice insurance will not cover it."

Covering the cost out of pocket would not be easy, so from the beginning, I suggested settling the case, but the state declined to settle. They were adamant that I should come to the hearing and face the consequences. The saying is true that misfortunes never come alone. The insurance not only declined to cover my legal fees, but they also refused to continue medical coverage, despite not paying a single dollar for litigation. So not only did I have to win the case, but the decision would come immediately on the day of the hearing; otherwise, I would lose any malpractice coverage.

Most insurance companies had already declined coverage, and hospitals stopped admission privileges. It was wave upon wave of torture, happening one after the other. With every mail I opened, I was expecting more bad news. I spent days preparing for the case, and at night, restful sleep was impossible. Prayer and preparation were the only consolidations I had. Restlessness and tiredness were apparent on my face, and I looked much older and fragile. I was worried about my health and what would happen if I died, mainly because my children were small and needed my support. There was no way out except to go and fight for justice.

Instinctively, Jeff examined the setting. Representatives from various government agencies were sitting in the room and on the outskirts of the hall that surrounded the central hearing area. Jeff introduced himself to the assembly and inquired about their acquaintance, as it might reveal their intentions.

Before the meeting commenced, witnesses were segregated in an adjacent room, but the prosecutor, the attorney for the state, kept Mr. Brady in the hearing room. Jeff immediately objected as Mr. Brady was also a witness, and his witness testimony could be adulterated. The prosecutor insisted, but the hearing council agreed with the defense. Mr. Brady was compelled to sit in a separate room. I wondered why the prosecutor was so unjust.

This emergency hearing took place before a three-member committee consisting of a physician, a nurse practitioner, and a pharmacist. The hearing commenced with an opening statement from the prosecutor. She appeared angry as she outlined allegations of overprescribing and dangerously prescribing pain medications. She projected the complaint as if this were a pill mill operation.

The defense denied the allegations, although carefully admitted some documentation deficiencies, primarily because of the electronic medical record (EMRs). There was no need to talk about documentation. Still, we showed that we were remorseful and thoughtful. Accepting deficiency in the documentation was our humility so we could work together to remove any weaknesses.

In the past, doctors' medical documentation meant scribbling a few lines in the patient's chart. It was often difficult to transfer that information to another doctor, as the handwriting was difficult to understand. To stay current, we bought electronic medical records (EMR), but the technology was new and consequently carried multiple glitches.

We realized the deficiency in the technology and so we partly used it to write our notes, while hoping future updates would unravel issues.

Therefore, part of the documentation was through EMR, and part was kept in paper format for every patient. If we received a request for any patient transfer, we would send both charts to the referring physician so that the receiving physician would get complete information to carry out the continuity of care.

Mr. Brady came to the office with a subpoena to acquire all medical records a few months prior to the hearing. He ordered all forms of documents, including everything on the computer and the paper charts. He likely didn't know much about EMR, as he wanted everything from the computer to be printed out, and he got all the paper charts. My staff printed patients' records in all possible formats, like progress notes, SOAP notes, or outline notes form. The electronic medical record was designed to include information taken from prior notes and might not change over time. There was no time even to think that the bulk of redundant information would be misleading.

EMR has loaded templates, meaning prewritten notes that the doctor might use while writing the notes. As ordered, we printed it in different formats, as well as printing out the templates. It was interesting that they did not bother to ask for a written summary on these records. I was confident they would call me to elaborate and discuss all these things, but nothing happened to me except that they wanted me to face the hearing.

The prosecutor's body language predicted she had already concluded the outcome of this matter and did not want to work with me to develop any sympathy that might lessen punishment.

After opening statements, the case proceeded with the prosecutor calling Mr. Brady as a witness. He was the chief investigator in the case and had experience with the police department; but he had no medical training or knowledge. After he was sworn in, Mr. Brady presented a journal in which he had tabulated all the prescriptions of controlled medications by my office in the last six months.

The recorded journal gave no background information, such as the reason or purpose for the prescriptions or the patient's length of time on medications. Was there a change in medicines over time? How were these medications started, and why? Was there any consultation with a specialist? How were these medications affecting the physical functioning of these patients? Were there any side effects? Was the provider asked to explain why these medications were prescribed? What happened to those patients who took those medications? Was there any sign of abuse or diversion? These details were not explained. The register was merely a compilation of medicines.

In cross-questioning, my attorney asked Mr. Brady if he had tried to find out why these medications were prescribed; he said no. When asked if he had consulted with anyone, he revealed the name of an ENT doctor, Dr. Stephen Cooper, who was his co-investigator. Dr. Cooper had informed the state that the medication was wrongly prescribed. This was the first time his name was revealed to us. The prosecutor, by law, was required to disclose his finding but had kept it secret.

As a matter of justice, when a case mainly stands on someone's opinion, then that person should either be brought as an expert witness so the defense can cross-examine the testimony, or the findings should be revealed to the defense prior to the trial. Further, a decision should not be based on a single opinion, as the opinion may not establish a standard of care. I could not understand at that time why they had tried to keep him secret.

One of the allegations was that many prescriptions were written from a Wilmington office, so Mr. Brady was asked about that allegation. He responded, "That was an error."

"Then, as retrieved from the transcription," my attorney said, "your investigation went from June 24, 2011, until August of 2011."

"Yes."

"From June 24, 2011, to August 2011, did you at any point pick up the phone or in-person speak with Dr. Niaz as to what his position was, as it related to the allegations?"

"No."

"Now, when the complaint was filed, as I understand it, you did talk to Dr. Niaz, and you told him that it was very important that he send a letter to the medical board, and he was to respond to the files that you were subpoenaing. Is that correct?"

"Yes."

"And certainly, the letter he sent was fairly extensive. Would you agree with that?"

"Yes."

"On page 1 of this letter, Dr. Niaz states at the very bottom: 'First, let me convey that we are extremely strict about patient compliance, drug abuse, and drug diversion. We randomly check patients' urine toxicology levels at our office, and the technician physically goes in the restroom to ensure that the specimen is genuinely collected from the patient. The specimen is then sent to Ameritox, our lab vendor, for confirmation and a titration study that shows the actual level of the medication in the patients' system. To further ensure patient compliance, we also perform pills counts on the prescribed medication.' And you were aware that the claim that he made he did on his patients. Is that correct?"

"Yes."

"Looking on page 2 of the letter. Dr. Niaz goes on to say, 'In response to these concerns, the patient, David, noted in the Pharmacist's Complaint, never received double prescription written double from our practice. If you have any prescription which is double, please forward to me. If a pharmacist had noticed any such incident, he/she should call me and report to me. Prior to this complaint, I have not been notified by any pharmacist that our office is writing two prescriptions (doubling a prescription), one for cash and the other for insurance. Consequently, we also understand that many pharmacies become crowded.' My question to you: Did you ever send him, at any point, examples of the double prescription that was allegedly made?"

"The double prescription was the two hundred written on the same day, the two hundred to be filled with Medicaid, and the forty pills extra to be paid with cash at another pharmacy. That was the double."

That is what the investigators considered "double." That showed a lack of knowledge and awareness of prescription laws. Legally, this was the way a prescriber had to write any prescription where the insurance had set a limit on the amount of medicine. The prescriber had to write two prescriptions, one that covered the medicine within the boundary of coverage and the remaining prescribed separately. These were not double prescriptions! The limit set by an insurance company is not the limit set by the FDA or CDC and cannot restrict a patient, if medically and therapeutically indicated.

The upper limit of medication coverage by the insurance could be based on economics. Therefore, medication quantity limit is an insurance coverage limit. Since these medications do not have ceiling effects, and patients may develop significant tolerances, many patients may need a much higher dosage than the insurance-set limit. Mr. Brady's explanation showed a lack of knowledge. This was profoundly serious, as the co-investigator to whom he referred as a consultant also did not know. So, the entire investigation team selected by the prosecution lacked the knowledge of governing laws related to pain management.

Question: "Well, Dr. Niaz goes on to say in the second paragraph of the letter: 'It is true that prescriptions sometimes cross the limit regarding quantity allowed by their respective insurances. In that instance, the patient has the right to fill the remaining of the prescription by their secondary insurances or may even pay cash. We cannot, medically speaking, force a patient to take medications within their insurance budgets. In such circumstances, one prescription is covered by the amount allowed by the insurance company and the remaining by other resources.' Did you ever investigate as to whether or not that was permissible?"

Answer: "That is what happens in a lot of situations where people have private insurances. Sometimes doctors do write more than one insurance company will allow. But, in regard to the Medicaid issue, that is a state regulation, and part of my duties as an officer of the state is to pass regulatory violations along to other agencies within the state."

This answer was critical, as this was the foundation of overprescriptions. There was no limit set by Medicaid or Medicare as to how much medication doctors can prescribe. Insurance limits set by Medicaid or Medicare Managed Care Organization (MCO) had nothing to do with how much medication a patient could take. Medication dosage is determined based on studies that are conducted in phase II of medical research. As written in a leading medical journal:

> Determining the optimal dosage is an important step in
> the development of any drug, as it will provide a basis to

demonstrate the effectiveness of that drug at different dosage levels. This determination is mainly attempted in phase II, notably by means of dose-response studies, but it is obvious that data obtained at every stage in the life of the drug will provide a better approach to dosage recommendations. Several examples are discussed. (*Rev Med Interne,* 1986 Nov, Spec No:21–7)

The FDA determines the dosage of a medication based on research and the insurance providers, including Medicaid and Medicare, and may set an upper limit of the quantity of a specific medicine allowed in a month. If the prescribing amount is higher, then a patient must pay out of pocket or use secondary insurance. Therefore, the statement by the investigator at the hearing indicated his lack of knowledge, which led to what I perceived—and will note again—as an agenda more akin to a "witch hunt."

Based on Mr. Brady's own words, "In regards to the Medicaid issue, that's a state regulation, and part of my duties as an officer of the state is to pass regulatory violations along to other agencies within the state." This comment indicated that no one from the state who was involved with this case understood the prescription law.

The questioning continued with the chief prosecutor.

Jeff said, "Let's go on. You indicated that the physicians, such as Dr. Niaz, should—if he believes 240 pills is necessary, which is forty pills more than the limit that Medicaid will reimburse—should call up and ask for prior authorizations for the increase. Is that your testimony?"

"Yes."

"And did you communicate that to Dr. Niaz—that that is what he should have done?"

"He was—from the conversation I had with Dr. Niaz—I believe he was aware of what these regulations were."

"OK, let's look at what he said in the very next paragraph with 240 that he was doing. He goes on to say, 'In fact'—meaning the 240—'this is what the pharmacies are compelling us to do; [for example], if the quantity of medication crosses the limit set by a specific insurance, the pharmacy fills on to the limited quantity set forth by the insurance company, and for the remaining quantity, the pharmacy requires another prescription of the same medicine to fill the rest of the medicine. In another example, if I write 150 quantities of medication and the insurance covers 120, they will fill only 120 and then ask the patient to bring in another prescription for the remaining thirty pills. This is a standard procedure.' Did you check with the pharmacies to see whether Dr. Niaz was accurate, and that's what he has to do when he thinks the patient needs more medication regarding pills than the secondary source for reimbursement?"

"No."

"Now, the next paragraph, I believe, [addresses] what you testified to was Dr. Niaz's knowledge as to getting prior approval from Medicaid. I'm just going to read to you.

"'The pharmacist also raised a concern about why we don't get approval from the insurance company for the remaining quantity. We do try regularly, but generally, they deny. I am enclosing for your review a recent attempt to get a prior authorization approval of a Fentanyl patch on one patient by Medicaid. They denied it because it crossed the limit set by Medicaid. So, when the insurance companies are not offering coverage, the patient has the right to seek medical treatment beyond their insurance limits.'"

Jeff continued with a question: "Did you ever take that into account, that Dr. Niaz specifically wrote in here that 'I tried to get prior approval, and Medicaid wouldn't give it to reimburse the patient, but the patient was entitled to get the medication I thought, as his pain management doctor, he needed'? Did you take that into account before a complaint was filed?"

"No."

Another concern noted in the complaint was that prescriptions may have two or three handwritings. Jeff continued from the letter I wrote to respond to complaints raised by the state.

"'Legally speaking, all controlled orders are required to be written on tamper-proof paper. We went extra lengths in this endeavor. We were not only using tamper-proof paper, but we also placed a raised seal that puts the stamp of our office locations on the prescription to ensure prescriptions were issued from our office. Carbon copies of orders were also placed in the patient's chart for future reference.' Mr. Brady, were you aware that he used tamper-proof prescriptions when he wrote prescriptions to his patients?"

"Yes."

Jeff continued reading from the letter. "'Finally, writing the name of a pharmacy on the prescription is to ensure that the same pharmacy fills the prescription, but sometimes, one pharmacy does not carry the medicine that was prescribed. We then end up writing the name of another pharmacy, but I am sure this is within the legal rights of the medical profession. All of our patients taking pain medications are required to sign a pain contract, and in the pain contract, they have to give us the name of the pharmacy that will fill their prescriptions, but sometimes, due to a shortage of medicine by one pharmacy, we have to allow a patient to go to another pharmacy.' Did you realize that was his explanation—why, at times, he would write a second prescription with the name of the pharmacy on it?"

"Yes. And then I would always see on pharmacy contracts; it would have maybe a primary pharmacy and a secondary pharmacy listed."

Questioning Mr. Brady continued.

"Now, looking at this letter, am I not correct that Dr. Ma [vice president of Union Hospital] states, point-blank, that he was asked by Dr. Niaz to write this letter describing his assumption of patients from Dr. Shah, who had his medical license in Maryland revoked on May 2, 2011? Correct?"

"Yes."

"And then the last sentence in that paragraph, he says about Dr. Niaz: 'His responsiveness helped to avoid an inevitable backlog in primary care offices and the emergency department.' Correct?"

"Yes."

Dr. Ma's letter was submitted to the Delaware Licensing Board to be clear that we did not start medications. Still, we inherited and were trying to manage them, as leaving the patient without a provider would force them to go to the street to acquire drugs.

The letter stated,

I was asked by Dr. Muhammed Arif Niaz to write this letter describing his assumption of patients from Dr. Dinesh Shah, who had his medical license in Maryland revoked on May 2, 2011. Prior to revocation of Dr. Shah's license, he received more than one suspension of his license to prescribe controlled substances. During one of his suspensions, Union Hospital of Cecil County notified three providers in the area who treat chronic pain patients in an attempt to assist with the transition to new providers for Dr. Shah's patients. Dr. Muhammed Niaz was one of the providers who agreed to make accommodations to his schedule to accept these patients. His responsiveness helped to avoid the inevitable backlog in primary care offices and the emergency department.

Jeff then said, "There is a letter from Dr. Shah, which I know you do not have, and that's dated December 12, 2011, that states, 'To Whom It May Concern.' And if we look at the third paragraph, Dr. Shah says, 'Dr. Niaz was amongst the first doctor to accept as many as he could in his practice without any advance notice.' And he's talking about his patients after he was suspended. Correct?"

"Correct."

"Now, Dr. Niaz also specifically told you that his practice got busier as a result of Dr. Cooper and Dr. Shah getting their licenses revoked. You recall that testimony, correct?"

"Yes."

"So, you do recall that there were records in the file that specifically noted that Dr. Niaz discharged them. Correct?"

"Yes."

"Do you recall, as you sit here today, what the reason was for him to discharge them?"

"Noncompliance with their drugs."

"Is it fair to say this is not your first investigation?"

"This is not my first investigation, but this would be my first investigation with the doctor and a nurse overprescribing."

"And I guess it goes without saying, with your law enforcement background, you're not a nurse, or a doctor, or anything like that."

"Correct."

"And with your background and your experience, sir, you don't have any idea of how many pills per day somebody gets prescribed for Xanax, do you?"

"I have no medical training."

"The same for oxycodone. You don't know how many pills per day is appropriate for somebody with chronic pain."

"That's correct."

"So you have no way, sir, of telling this panel whether these amounts of drugs that were prescribed are actually more than what's acceptable, do you?"

"Sir, how the investigations proceeded when I was a medical investigator, the board—the executive director of the board—assigns a doctor to a case as a co-investigator; in this case, the doctor was Dr. Stephen Cooper."

Interestingly, Dr. Cooper was an ENT doctor, not a pain-management physician. He was a co-investigator and acted as an expert, and therefore, his findings should have been disclosed to the defense. Why were his name and findings kept secret?

Jeff went on. "When you met Nurse Practitioner Binkley and were talking about her speaking to you, you used the term 'us.' Was that just a general use, or was there somebody else with you when she was talking to you?"

"There was another investigator."

"OK. And do you recall, sir, you or the other investigator, telling Jean Binkley essentially that Dr. Niaz was throwing her under the bus?"

"I can't recall."

"Do you recall if, in general, you told Nurse Binkley that Dr. Niaz was pointing the finger at her?"

"I told her about the conversation I had with Dr. Niaz, that Dr. Niaz had planned to terminate her after he got his new nurse practitioner trained."

"And why would you tell her that, sir? Were you trying to get [her] to say something about Dr. Niaz?"

"I told her to tell the truth."

As my attorney continued questioning Mr. Brady, he asked him to discuss what happened the day he and the DEA agent came to my office.

"If we look at Exhibit 6 of the state's exhibits, which is the letter that Dr. Niaz signed, dated December 8, 2011, agreeing to revoke his license temporarily, do you see that investigator?"

"Yes" said Mr. Brady.

"And you specifically testified that by signing this, you made it clear that Dr. Niaz didn't agree that he had done anything wrong. Correct?"

"That is correct; it was voluntary."

"You say it's voluntary, but you showed up with a federal agent in Dr. Niaz's office. Is that fair?"

"I went to the office. The DEA agent came by his own volition. He wasn't driving along with me."

"OK. Both of you went. Dr. Niaz was in his office, seeing patients?"

"Correct."

"You went in there, and you told him or asked whether he would sign this voluntarily. Is that correct?"

"That's what the federal agent did."

"I will represent to you that when Dr. Niaz testified, he will say that he was told that it was in his best interest to sign this form. 'If not, I will make a criminal case against you.' Do you recall him saying that to Dr. Niaz?"

"Yes."

"And after hearing that statement from the federal agent— that it's in his best interest to sign it, and if he doesn't, the federal agent will make a criminal case against you—Dr. Niaz voluntarily signed this form. Correct?"

"After he spoke to his attorney, yes."

This was under oath; the chief state investigator had confirmed he'd threatened my nurse practitioner and me to sign DEA papers. This was one of the ways they brought their case. The following day, the *News Journal* featured that story on the front page, highlighting my voluntary surrender of my DEA license, which implied acceptance of guilt.

Obviously, the DEA agent and the state investigator coming simultaneously to my office to suspend my state and federal licenses could not have been a coincidence. In fact, it was a well-designed plan, intended to portray an acceptance of guilt. The hearing officers probably read those articles and had already established the impression that I was guilty.

A few weeks before this rude intrusion into my life, newspapers were publishing articles about doctors prescribing pain medications indiscriminately. The whole case was based on assumptions that doctors were writing excessively large doses of pain medications without therapeutic indications.

Cross-questioning continued. "Can you tell me whether any of these patients were on similar drugs or greater drugs before the time Dr. Niaz took over their care?"

"Not off of this record," Mr. Brady said.

"My last question on these charts—can you tell me whether any of these patients in this chart ever gave a fraudulent prescription that somehow the pharmacy filled, by looking at this document?"

"I don't know."

"Now, I noticed that you don't have any notes on you. Do you have any notes that you took of these interviews?"

"No."

"So all your testimony as to what these people have said is based on your memory. Is that correct?"

"Based off my report."

"Did you bring your report with you today?"

"I don't have it here with me in this room."

"Is there any particular reason why you did not bring your report with you in order to make sure that whatever you testified to was accurate?"

"No."

"Well, do you have notes, or do you just have a report?"

"I have a report."

"And the report is written from notes that you took originally?"

"Yes."

"Where are those original notes?"

"Disposed of."

Next, the prosecutor presented the pharmacist, who they claimed started the complaints. The prosecutor asked, "Why did you make the complaints?"

"I wanted to express just a concern. I said, not saying there was any wrongdoing, just we noticed excessive amounts of narcotic prescriptions for various different people."

"Now, in the complaint that you made to the Division for Professional Regulation, you expressed a concern that patients were coming with a prescription for a certain number of pain pills written for Medicaid and then a certain number for cash."

"I don't remember that."

"Please take a look at that. The redacted names are patient names."

"OK. I don't remember them all. But I know some doctors will write—if Medicaid allows—they have a limit, two hundred a month of certain pain medications. And if the patient needs 240, sometimes they will write one prescription for two hundred, one for forty, so they can—because you have to split them up that way. Usually, what we like to see, that way it kind of covers our butt if the doctor writes on one 'cash because of the Medicaid limit' or—you know, so that you can do that."

"Now, did you ever have an occasion to call Dr. Niaz and talk to him or anybody in his office about your concerns?"

"Not specifically about the amount of prescriptions coming up."

"OK. And you said some red flags were up, but you made it very clear in your testimony during direct examination that, as a pharmacist, you can't say Dr. Niaz or anybody in his office did anything wrong, and you can't say that they wrote excessively. All you can say is that you had some red flags because of the amount of prescriptions that were coming in. Correct?"

"Right."

"But you are aware, based on your experience, that there are certain severely chronically ill patients who are pain-medication patients that do come in from pain clinics that have prescriptions similar to what was written for these patients. Correct?

"Correct."

"And as a pharmacist, when a doctor, for whatever reason, feels that a patient needs more than the maximum reimbursable amount by Medicaid, you want that doctor to do exactly what was done in this case, and that is, put two hundred down for the Medicaid, and then the second prescription, to make sure he puts down 'cash.' That way you're covered, and he's covered."

"Right."

"And finally, you have no idea whether those patients were former patients of another physician that he was seeing, that they were seeing for pain, whose license was revoked. Correct?"

"Right. I have no way to know."

"By the same token, did you ever speak on the phone to Dr. Niaz about the problem that you thought existed?"

"No, I didn't pose it—I didnt want to assume it was a definite problem."

As I've mentioend previously, for continuity of patient care in Maryland, I wrote a letter to pharmacies in Maryland, informing them of my unrestricted status and to please continue to fill the prescriptions written from the Maryland office. It was outrageous and shocking to see that the prosecutor had collected the letter and put that in the hearing as evidence, implying I was still writing prescriptions after the emergency suspension of my controlled substance registration. This diverted the fact that the allegations raised in the state of Delaware would not be applicable in other states, or they were trying to incite the state of Maryland.

After the testimony of the pharmacist, the nurse practitioner was called. Her statement was extensive, but nowhere in the declaration did the prosecutor present any evidence of overprescription or double prescription. Apparently, the prosecutor was trying to understand the charts, which should have been done before the hearing. It was a very nebulous discussion, and instead of focusing on the allegations, the prosecutor questioned aimlessly. After the nurse practitioner, it was my turn to testify.

CHAPTER 5

After the oath, the prosecutor started her questioning by presenting an article that focused on drug overuse in the nation. She gave it as evidence that doctors were overprescribing pain medications. Interestingly, that same article noted that patient pain was undertreated, and patients were suffering due to this undertreatment. Tragically, research showed that 50–70 percent of patients died from moderate to severe pain, despite the availability of opioids and other therapies to control pain.

I explained what a physician went through in treating patients' pain. Pain is challenging to treat, partly because there is no specific parameter to measure. It is subjective and may not have any underlying pathology. I referred to the first published in 2008 by the Federation of State Medical Boards, which emphasized the importance of treating pain. Pain was added to the list of vital signs, which included blood pressure, pulse, and respiration. These vital signs are measurable, but pain is subjective and cannot be measured. Often, a doctor has to rely on a patient's statement. Furthermore, the Federation of State Medical Boards also indicated, based on research, that the risk from controlled substance was low.

As a result of that research, many doctors began prescribing narcotic pain medications, which resulted in millions of people becoming dependent on pain medications. Addiction and dependency are two different clinical conditions that nonprofessionals commonly think are interchangeable. Dependency simply means a person has taken a remedy for an extended period, and a sudden stoppage would spark withdrawal signs and symptoms. Dependency generally does not lead to loss of control. In other words, a person can have control over the amount of pain medication taken in and would not seek out illegal drugs.

Addiction, on the other hand, implies that a person has lost control and may end up buying illegal drugs or using illicit means or engaging in dangerous activities. Often, a layman interchanges these words; for example, drinking coffee regularly in the morning results in a caffeine dependency that is not an addiction, but people call it caffeine addiction.

Switching gears, the prosecutor asked about Dr. Shah.

"Do you know why Dr. Shah was suspended?" she asked.

"It was in the news and nothing to do with me," I answered.

"Why did you accept his patients?"

I indicated the request by Union Hospital. "As they were overwhelmed by the influx of patients who were on the extremely high dosage of pain medications for an extended period, there was a need for a medical provider." I referred to the letter written by the regional hospital, stating that they requested three primary care doctors to accept these patients. "Further, many patients were discharged from the practice due to noncompliance."

By her questions, it appeared to me that she was trying to link me with Dr. Shah and was trying to prove these patients were addicted and should not have been accepted. She opened a chart and asked, "Why did you choose oxycodone [as] the pain [medication for] this patient?"

I asked her, "Why do you think oxycodone should not be given to this patient? The patient came to the practice with a high dosage of oxycodone, and we were gradually reducing medications."

She looked at me as if I had no knowledge of medicine; she spoke loudly when she said, "Because oxycodone contains Tylenol, and this patient has hepatitis C."

I was shocked by her confidence in the wrong information. I responded very politely, "Oxycodone does not have Tylenol."

She looked at the hearing panel, expecting they would intervene. In reality, even if the medicine has Tylenol (acetaminophen), it can still be used to treat pain in a hepatitis patient. These are places where caution is advised in the amount of acetaminophen and the status of hepatitis C and the liver. Many hepatitis C patients have zero viral loads, which means they may be cured. Still, a blood test would show positive for hepatitis C.

At this point, I asked, "Out of these charts, can you please point out one chart where I increased any pain medications, let alone overprescribed?"

She failed to indicate a chart where I had increased medications. This was significant because the basis of this case resided on overprescription. The evidence did not support the allegations; the whole matter was based on assumptions, followed by a witch hunt. She decided not to go further, so cross-questioning ended.

When evaluating appropriate pain management, the most essential part of the evaluation should be who started the pain medications? What was the indication? Is there a supporting pathology or a clinical condition requiring pain medications? Has there been an analysis of how the patient was affected (e.g., functioning, daily activities, able to perform profitable operations, mood, behavior, mentation, driving and operating abilities, and relation to other people, including family members)? Were patients obtunded or overdosed? Considering the development of tolerance, how long have these patients been on this medication? Have patients been with one provider all along, or were they transferred from other doctors? If they were transferred, why were they transferred? What level of care did they receive from their previous physician? Were any patients guilty of selling drugs? Was there been any prescription forgery, drug abuse, or diversion?

The prosecution's main focus was on doctors writing excessive pain medication prescriptions. The prosecutor had a journal where all the prescriptions written in the last six months were tabulated, which, according to her, was proof that the practice was writing excessive pain medications, like a pill mill.

My attorney, Jeff, began his cross-examination. He read a letter from the vice president of Union Hospital:

> I was asked by Dr. Muhammed A. Niaz to write this letter describing his assumption of patients from Dr. Dinesh Shah, who had his medical License in Maryland

revoked on May 2, 2011. Prior to revocation of Dr. Shah's License, he received more than one suspension of his License to prescribe controlled substances. During one of his suspensions, Union Hospital of Cecil County notified three providers in the area who treat chronic pain patients in an attempt to assist with the transition to new providers for Dr. Shah. Muhammed Niaz was one of the providers who agreed to make accommodations to his schedule to accept these patients. His responsiveness helped to avoid the inevitable backlog in primary care offices and the emergency department.

Jeff then read a letter that I wrote to the state, explaining that the patients were accepted on humanitarian grounds, based upon the request of Union Hospital. From the letter, Jeff pointed out that Dr. Denish Shaw's name was misspelled. In the letter, I spelled it as Dr. Denish "Shah." This was important, as the prosecutor attempted to show this as an indication that Dr. Shah was my friend or had a working relationship with me.

Since the prosecutor did not ask any questions related to patient care, we felt it was essential to show patient charts. The state alleged four patients' charts represented a model of the alleged overprescription scheme. Investigators tabulated medicines written over many months. We disclosed errors in tabulating patients' medications; the errors were gross. In fact, the data presented was 50 percent overstated. The prosecutor's expert lacked practical knowledge or experience to understand medicines dispensed. They at least compared the prescriptions written by the office with the pharmacy profile to ensure the exact amount of medications were delivered to patients.

Also, out of four patients, the first patient's medication record was merged with another patient's record bearing the same name.

For the second patient, medications were recorded for six months, although I saw that patient only once, and at that visit, the patient was discharged. Investigators should have seen who wrote those prescriptions instead of just labeling me. The prosecutor was shocked to learn that I only saw that patient once; in fact, I discharged the patient at that very same visit.

The third patient was a teacher, referred from the methadone clinic with a history of heroin addiction. She was seeking buprenorphine treatment, replacing methadone, to allow her to better perform her work-related activities. She was detoxified from methadone to buprenorphine. Her treatment induction was successful. She had tachycardia, which she linked to generalized anxiety disorder, and was advised a short course of benzodiazepine to settle her tachycardia. She was also referred to a cardiologist and psychiatrist. The manifestation of tachycardia was life-threatening. Therefore, an EKG was performed, which did not indicate any specific etiology. She was subsequently switched to beta-blockers, which resolved her symptoms.

The state raised serious allegations that the combination of Xanax (benzodiazepine) with buprenorphine was an absolute contraindication and was against the standard of care. The combination was considered lethal and illegal to prescribe. Apparently, the prosecutor's (or whoever they used as the expert) knowledge was based on the *Physicians' Desk Reference* (PDR) report, which reported a few patients had shot this combination intravenously and died. Therefore, the PDR advised caution. PDR is written to provide a guideline and is not a standard of care.

No wonder, with the opioid epidemic raging all across the country, the state seemed eager to show punishment as a notice to other providers. Unfortunately, their haste and their lack of properly trained medical investigators were now something I had to answer, and that would have a huge negative impact on my life, both personally and professionally.

What the state failed to understand was that managing a patient with an addiction posed multiple risks because the patient might have various underlying medical issues, which are sometimes overlooked due to the overshadowing addiction. Once detoxified, some patients may manifest other medical signs and symptoms. Similarly, treating patients with pain requires taking a risk but analyzing the risk-to-benefit ratio. A patient who has chronic obstructive pulmonary disease (COPD) and requires narcotic pain medications could lead to suppressed breathing, due to added underlying pulmonary disease. So, a layman reviewing patient care could label it as egress from the standard of care. The clinical challenge for a physician is, if a patient has COPD and needs pain medication, should the doctor withhold any narcotic prescription and let the patient suffer? There are millions of patients in America who have COPD, and they are taking narcotic pain medication. Pain medications have made a big difference in the lives of many patients. The patient who was a teacher, previously described, started continually working after her treatment because the procedure was successful. In fact, one of the three-member panel of judges indicated that she had used this combination.

At the end of my testimony, I decided to go through the list of medications tabulated by the investigator in the journal related to these patients. The nurse practitioner helped me point out the mistakes in the data collection. In a short period, we were able to show that most of the listed medicines were inaccurate, and the state did not offer a rebuttal. It was clear that the prosecutor now had a different view of this case.

After my testimony ended, it was time for the hearing panel to make their decision. Waiting for their decision was the most nervous moment of my life! Overwhelming fear took over in my mind. If I lost this case, it would end my career.

After the end of the hearing, the panel had to deliberate their decision. I was panicky and uncomfortable because the panel was not made up of pain doctors—one was a surgeon, one was a nurse practitioner, and one was a pharmacist. They might rule on the side of the state. The foundation of this litigation was based on this journal with tabulated medications listings, which looked enormous. That was projected in the media as a pill mill. The breaking news highlighted in the media was that the current epidemic of drug usage, particularly among teenagers, causing addiction and increased mortality, violence, and school dropout rates was linked to my practice. The prosecutor demanded that pain doctors be punished for countering this nationwide drug epidemic.

The panel was in discussion for nearly an hour. We were able to hear their discussion but were not allowed to interfere or say anything. The pharmacist on the panel expressed deficiency in diagnosis because he did not see the form that he stated was required to diagnose an ADD disorder. So, as he asked the other judges, how could they prescribe ADD medications? I was silent, but my mind was protesting that this patient came from another practice and was taking medication for this condition for an extended period. I did not know how to convey to them that the form related to the ADD symptoms record was mainly designed for pediatric patients. The form was only a guideline, not of any regulatory importance.

Similarly, the doctor on the panel raised a concern: why did they prescribe Xanax on a patient who was on buprenorphine? Fortunately, the nurse practitioner replied, as she had experienced using this combination, "I did it in my practice." The discussion was based mainly on theoretical knowledge since they did not practice pain management. The debate continued back and forth, with the panel raising concerns and discussing among themselves. After back and forth for about an hour, the panel ruled in my favor. Their decision was unanimous. As a result, the panel ordered the secretary of state to reverse their earlier decision regarding my license and said that the secretary of state was in a vacuum and could not fully comprehend the situation.

I breathed a huge sigh of relief. It was finally over, and I no longer had to dread losing my medical malpractice insurance, which would have terminated if I had lost this case. My situation had become even more demoralizing when hospitals pulled out; most insurance providers also left. Thus, my practice of medicine would have been nearly impossible. The hearing panel's decision meant a restored life for me and left me feeling more hopeful.

As required, the hearing panel sent their findings to the secretary of state. Summary of the hearing panel's findings and recommendations included:

1. The DEA agent presented Dr. Niaz with the voluntary surrender form; Mr. Brady heard the agent tell Dr. Niaz, "it is in your best interest to sign this, and if you don't, I will bring a criminal case against you."
2. Mr. Brady testified that after consulting with Dr. Cooper, the co-investigator in this matter, he determined that the investigative files should be sent to the attorney general's office for prosecution.
3. The panel could not find that Dr. Niaz wrote any double prescriptions.
4. The panel finds there was a large influx of patients at the request of Union Hospital to provide continuity of care.

5. The panel finds that there were several factual errors in the state's complaints. Errors include in tabulation, mixing two patients as one, as well as counting.

The panel unanimously concluded and requested of the Secretary of State,

> they cannot find that substantial evidence exists to support a finding that the suspension of the registrations of Dr. Niaz or Ms. Binkley is warranted to address any imminent danger to the public health or safety and the Panel recommends the Secretary dissolve the temporary suspension of their controlled substance licenses.

The decision by the panel was a recommendation to the secretary of state; the prosecutor had the right to write a rebuttal to the findings of the panel. The case was not over, as the prosecutor did write a rebuttal to uphold the earlier decision of suspension. She based her counterargument on the fact that the burden of proof was shifted to the defense to prove that the medical practice was prescribing safely.

It was outrageous; the prosecutor and the state should have been looking for facts, not just to win the case but to make headlines toward their role of helping with the current opioid crisis tha was hurting many. If the burden of proof rested on the defense, then it should have been stated accordingly before the hearing. Shouldn't they have looked to see if regulatory laws were violated? Was the practice of medicine according to the standard of care? Did any patient suffer any undue egress in medical care?

Putting the burden of proof on the defense, when multiple errors were clearly explained, based on factual evidence, highlighted the prosecutor's desire to make an example of this case to all other providers in Delaware who were providing care for pain management.

The health system in the USA performs very poorly in comparison with the health systems in similar countries. Though unhealthy substance use and education is America's number-one health problem, with regard to global ratings of health, with 1 being best and 37 being worst, the United

States ranks 36. This is according to the US Department of Health and Human Services, Office of the Surgeon General.

> Facing Addiction in America. The Surgeon General's Report on Alcohol, Drugs and Health

> Patients with acute and chronic pain in the United States face a crisis because of significant challenges in obtaining adequate care, resulting in profound physical, emotional, and societal costs. According to the Centers for Disease Control and Prevention, 50 million adults in the United States have chronic daily pain, with 19.6 million adults experiencing highimpact chronic pain that interferes with daily life or work activities. The cost of pain to our nation is estimated at between $560 billion and $635 billion annually. At the same time, our nation is facing an opioid crisis that, over the past two decades, has resulted in an unprecedented wave of overdose deaths associated with prescription opioids, heroin, and synthetic opioids. (https://www.ncbi.nlm.nih.gov/pmc/articles/PMC6311547)

There are multiple published reports of doctors prescribing less pain medication in the last decade. According to the CDC, Center for Disease and Prevention between 1988 and 1994 trend of prescription drug 39.1 percent, which is reduced 11.2 percent by 2015 to 2018. The health care cost, per capita, in 2019 showed the US spent $10,988, while the UK spent $4,653 per capita.

According to Delaware Division of Professional Regulation Updates 2019, the Delaware opioid-related overdose death rate is in the top five states in the USA per one hundred residents. A person suffering from pain has two options: either go to a doctor who can prescribe pain medications or go buy drugs off the street. Regulatory authorities taking actions on doctors who prescribe pain medication, which, in the past, was considered the fifth vital sign, has resulted in a massive transition of patients from the doctor's office to the street.

The term the prosecutor used in her rebuttal was "safe practice," as if the defendant failed to prove how the medical practice was safe. The word *safe* could have multiple meanings, For example, if a doctor prescribes insulin to a diabetic patient, the doctor takes a calculated risk that insulin can lower blood sugar. Can a doctor lose his or her license because the patient's blood sugar dropped? The doctor has to evaluate benefit versus harm, and if the provider concludes that medication would be more beneficial, a provider can advise the treatment. After all, patients have the autonomy, which is defined as the patient's right to make decisions about their medical care without their health care provider trying to influence the decision. Mainly, the entire litigation was based on chart review and medication counting. No outcome was discussed.

After a month's interval, the secretary of state issued an order that stated:

> Finally, the State argues that the burden of proof rests with Dr. Niaz and Ms. Binkley to refute the State's allegations of professional misconduct that pose an imminent danger to the public health or safety. The Secretary rejects the State's position as unsupported by law and precedent. However, much of the evidence presented in defense of the prescribing practices of Dr. Niaz and Ms. Binkley was "unrebutted" by the State at the post-deprivation Hearing.

CHAPTER 6

After the initial emergency hearing in December 2011, in which the hearing panel concluded against the allegations raised by the state, the secretary of state agreed with the hearing panel, and my controlled substance registration became active. The newspapers again published the news as a headline, announcing the decision of the secretary of state. At this point, I was expecting that the prosecutor would agree to settle the case.

The media inflamed the story by adding comments from related dignitaries as they asked the prosecutor to comment on the decision. The prosecutor's response was "no comment." To me, her comment sounded like the lull before the storm. The common understanding regarding the state going for any prosecution is that it's for the public interest. But with the newspaper highlighting my story, I was beginning to worry that the prosecutor might convert the litigations to a personal level, and it would become a matter of maintaining her own dignity and competence.

I thought the state had seen the true nature and circumstances of the complicated medical situation and would agree to settle the case. Instead, my fears became real—they *started looking for ways to win the case and make me an example*. So, the witch hunt continued.

After a few weeks passed, I got a call from my attorney. He informed me that the state had sent a subpoena requesting more charts. Accordingly, copies of the requested records, including both paper charts and printouts from the EMRs, were submitted, resulting in large bundles of papers. A few days later, the process continued. I thought about what exactly they were looking for, as they never bothered to communicate with me or ask me to write a summary on any patient record. Subpoenas kept appearing, one after the other, multiple times. Obviously, the state was looking to prove something.

On March 8, 2012, the state decided to come up with new allegations; they called it "Amendment Complaints."

In the Amendment Complaints, claims shifted from overprescription to inappropriate documentation and insufficient supervision of the nurse practitioner. The state needed a standard to prove deficiency in medical documentation, as there was no such legal standard established at that time. The only legal requirement was to have documentation regarding patient care. The state then created standards in medical documentation, based on the guidelines written in model policy by the Federation of State Medical Boards. One glaring omission, however, was that the state ignored the fact that the model policy was not yet implemented as a law by the Delaware Licensing Board. The policy was only a guideline, and deviation from the procedure was by no means illegal or considered as egress from medical practice.

Responsible Opioid Prescribing: A Physician's Guide by Dr. Scott M. Fishman (2007), published by the Federation of State Medical Boards, explains the model policy. In the book, Dr. Fishman wrote on page 3:

> Although the model policy represents the most concise consensus guidelines for the safe opioid prescribing until now, this document has not been translated into practical terms for clinical practice. Consequently, few physicians are familiar with these guidelines, and even fewer utilize them in their practice.

On page 81, it stated, "If this testing (urine toxicology) is employed, as in all therapeutic decisions, it must be used solely in the service of the patient best interests." On page 103, it stated, "The FSMB Model Policy does not set a standard of medical practice."

Unfortunately, to our detriment, during the emergency hearing before a three-member committee, we made a compassionate opening statement acknowledging our weakness related to electronic medical records but indicated these shortcomings were fixed and did not affect patient care in any way. An expert we hired, Dr. Abraham Kabazie, MD, medical director at the Institute for Pain Medicine, Western Pennsylvania Hospital, in Pittsburgh, also concurred. Documentation was never mentioned in any earlier allegations or investigations. This charge was made only after our self-disclosure to show we were conscious of flaws in the reporting and the announcemnt of our desired goal to improve any weakness. What we had offered as a gesture to conclude the case on mutual consensus motivated the prosecution to use our concession to win the case.

Briefly, the complaints focused on the physician's failure to supervise the nurse practitioner and that documented patients' notes were not written according to the model policy, which was not the law, nor was it the physician's responsibility to supervise the nurse practitioner. The nurse practitioner holds independent prescriptive authority. She was required to develop a working agreement with the doctor and to consult if needed. Another allegation was that the practice was overprescribing pain medications and even prescribing pain medications to pregnant patients, so children were born addicted to pain medication. Although there is no such term in medicine where children are born addicted, I wanted to see how they would prove that children were born addicted to pain medications; this also implied that pain medication given to a pregnant patient is a violation of the standard of care. Since the prosecutor indicated dangerous prescribing of pain medication, I expected they would bring some evidence of a bad outcome.

They wanted to be victorious. Their intentions were loud and clear.

The assessment needed to address the cumbersome records and the intricacies of the case swirled in my head, but I still continued to treat my Maryland patients, and the state continued to keep the hits coming my way.

Just two weeks before the hearing date, we received second amended allegations. In the second amendment, they added billing discrepancies, inferring fraud, as they alleged the office charged higher bills, while reiterating the same charges using different language, like improper supervision to the nurse practitioner and ethical fallacies in delivering services to the patient. I wondered if they were feeling insecure about proving earlier allegations, as they were enough to revoke any physician's license if confirmed in a hearing. They added more allegations that showed their skepticism and frustration.

The additional charges included allegations regarding overprescription, as they wrote: "In that he issued prescriptions for dangerous and/or narcotic drugs, other than for therapeutic or diagnostic purposes."

Additional allegations related to treatment were:

> To receive information from Respondent and to discuss the benefits, risks, and costs of appropriate treatment alternatives. ... Did not provide alternative treatment modalities, cost of treatment. ... in that he failed to use sound medical judgment, holding the best interests of his patients as paramount.

Complaints were also raised regarding keeping the medical records, as stated, "Rule 15.1.4 in that he intentionally failed to maintain records concerning the prescriptions for controlled substances he wrote for his patients."

The role in supervising the nurse practitioner in the delegation of medical care was reemphasized, as the complaint stated, "Rule 21.1.1 in that he failed to adequately supervise his employee nurse practitioners including but not limited to Binkley and other staff members."

Now, for the first time, the added complaints regarding medical billing stated, "During 2011, Respondent charged and billed patients and/or his staff provided."

It was devastating to know my office had to address issues that were previously not known, expected, or requested. We hardly had time to go through all the charts or the billing in depth. The task ahead was almost inconceivable. Still, we decided to accept the challenge, as the case had already put my practice in a deep hole financially, and my malpractice insurance denied my coverage due to the disciplinary nature, so further lingering would most likely bankrupt us.

To prepare a defense, we needed disclosures and findings of the experts from the state. No information related to any evidence was given from the state. We knew they had interrogated many of our employees. What was the outcome? At this point, to gather information, my defense attorney sent forty-seven questions related to disclosure to find out how they had reached these amended allegations. Surprisingly, they responded to only one item. To the rest of the discovery requests, they responded either "not applicable" or "Objection, this request is unduly burdensome and overly broad and are beyond the scope of discovery permitted in administrative proceedings. In addition, the documents sought, if they exist, are not discoverable as they constitute work-product prepared by investigators used by government attorneys in anticipation of litigation; are exempt from disclosure pursuant to FOIA, and are subject to a qualified governmental privilege."

In our opinion, this use of legal precedent and jargon did not seem equitable to our ability to defend our position. The only item they partially disclosed was the following:

1. State the name and present or last-known address of each person whom you expect to call as an expert witness at trial, as to each person named.

> Dr. Ward will testify as an expert witness against the Respondents. Dr. Ward is certified by the American Board of Medical Specialties in Physical Medicine and Rehabilitation and Pain Medicine and is an expert in both fields of practice. Dr. Ward is expected to testify that Dr. Niaz engaged in unprofessional conduct and unethical practices in violation of the statutes and regulations as alleged in the State's Complaints and in violation of the standard of care in the practice of pain management and that Ms. Binkley engaged in unprofessional conduct and unethical practices in violation of the statutes and regulations as alleged in the State's Complaints and in violation of the standard of care in connection with the practice of pain management. Dr. Ward's opinions will be based on his Review of records. Dr. Ward will also testify all the allegations as raised by the State and allegations were included in the answers.

Also disclosed:

> The fee schedule for Dr. Ward as an expert medical examiner, door to door service is $500.00 per hour or a total of $4000.00 a day. The fees do not include travel expenses or hotel expenses.

The legal standard is to disclose any deficiency or that the expert's opinion be disclosed to the defense *before* the hearing. The statement above confirmed that Dr. Ward had already reviewed the relevant charts and had provided an opinion to the state, which the state then had disclosed to us, with the indicated service fees paid to Dr. Ward at $500 per hour for whatever time he took to review the charts. What we were expecting was simply the reporting of any specific deficiency found. His purpose should not have been to prove the state's allegations. As an expert, he should have been neutral. There was no disclosure of the deficiencies mentioned by Dr. Ward.

It is very important to note that this declaration of Dr. Ward's opinion was given to us about one month before the hearing. Now, we were playing a guessing game and thinking of all possible avenues. Earlier, the licensing board had sent me certified letters with signature required. I had to go to the post office to sign and receive those letters, which indicated some findings. These were related to patients treated in Christiana Hospital. I was the attending physician of Christiana Hospital and was aware of these patients.

> J M. was pronounced dead in the Emergency Room at Christiana Hospital on 10/28/2010 for an adverse drug reaction. Williams was a patient of Dr. Muhammed Niaz and prescribed medications and narcotics. Dr. Niaz's medication treatment plan might have had an adverse effect upon the patient and been an attributing cause to her death.

The allegation was not based on any fact. The truth was that the patient was discharged from my practice over six months before her death.

She had received some pain medications, as she had developed shingles, accompanied with painful neuropathy. She had multiple comorbid conditions and was also seeing a psychiatric doctor. She was commuting from Wilmington, a town far from my practice, so she requested to move to a practice more convenient to her commute. As per request, she was discharged, and her records were transferred to her new physician. She was under treatment of her new physician for over six months before she committed suicide.

In reviewing records from the subsequent physicians, we discovered she died due to suicide, and the postmortem report indicated the cause of death was psychiatric medications, not any pain medication prescribed. Obviously, pain medications do not stay in the body for over six months, even if they would try to link the circumstance to pain medications prescribed from our office. The missing link in our learning of this alleged charge was that the state, or the prosecutor, never communicated with us. If they had done their due diligence of standard practice, we could have shown them the truth and have avoided the situation of putting forth an allegation without any due process.

Description of Complaint

A- G, male, age 51, was pronounced dead at Christiana Hospital due to respiratory failure. This person was a patient of Dr. Niaz. It is believed that Dr. Niaz's treatment plan of medication and narcotic was a contributing factor to the patient's death.

The fact was, this patient had full-blown AIDS and suffered from opportunistic infections. He stayed in the hospital for over one month, under treatment, before he died. Death certificate did not indicate pain medications as a contributing factor leading to his death; in fact, narcotic drugs were not even mentioned in the death certificate. He died due to AIDS-causing severe infections and pneumonia.

Description of Complaint

M Hal, female, age 50, was pronounced dead in the emergency room of Christiana Hospital on 9/7/2011. This person had been under the care of Dr. Niaz. It is believed that Dr. Niaz's medical treatment plan of medication and narcotics was a contributing factor in the patient's death.

Again, there was not even a grain of truth in this allegation. The patient was never seen in the office. The only link we could find was that his insurance card listed the primary care physician as Dr. Niaz. The investigator never bothered to find out how I was involved in his care. It is feasible that he randomly chose my name when he applied for insurance.

Description of Complaint

S. K Jr, male, age 41 was pronounced dead in the Emergency Room of Christiana Hospital on 1/21/2011 of cardio-respiratory failure. This patient was under the care of Dr. Niaz. It is believed that Dr. Niaz's treatment plan of medication and narcotics was a contributing factor to the patient's death.

Again, I never saw this patient. So anything related to his care linked to me was absurd. We explored his records from the hospital. He had multiple comorbid conditions, including severe cardiac failure, morbid obesity, obstructed sleep apnea, arthritis, lumbago, and disc disease. How I was blamed is beyond my comprehension. It was evident the state was desperate to win the case, to set an example for other pain doctors.

Generally, patients with multiple medical diagnoses have conditions that manifest with severe pain. Often, they required narcotic and non-narcotic pain medications. Since narcotic pain medications develop tolerance quickly and need a higher dosage to control their pain, most non-narcotic pain medications are commonly used as a nonsteroidal anti-inflammatory drug (NSAID) like ibuprofen or naproxen carry significant side effects and therefore may not be appropriate in many patients. A physician has to treat patients' pain to ease the suffering. These patients are at high risk due to multiple comorbid conditions. One may blame pain medications as a reason for their deaths. Still, I would argue that even if we agreed that pain medicines contributed to their demise, what would have been the options of a patient suffering from multiple medical problems, including pain? Should a doctor let the patient be agonized with pain or reduce suffering?

The examples cited above regarding the tragic loss of life were rife with gross errors, and it suggested a lack of preparation for the prosecution to provide accurate documentation. We could not figure out how they would produce these patients' records as evidence to prove their allegations. Was there some missing link?

As previously noted, the investigator who came to the office was Mr. Brady, whose background was as a police investigator. He had no medical training or experience. So who was the expert supervising their investigation? The only person officially disclosed was Mr. Brady. While searching transcripts from the previous emergency hearing, we realized that Mr. Brady mentioned, during the cross-examination, the name of Dr. Stephen Cooper, an ENT doctor, as their expert investigator. Though Dr. Cooper did not have any background in pain management, we expected his findings would be disclosed. Why was the state keeping his testimony secret? We also hoped they would bring him as an expert witness in the first trial, but the prosecutor did not even mention his name, as if he didn't exist.

Dr. Francisco Ward, who was retained as an expert by the state, was a doctor of osteopathic medicine (DO), while I am MD, doctor of medicine. His training was in physical medicine and rehabilitation, while my training was in internal medicine. He achieved a certificate in pain medicine, while I hold a certificate in pain management. His pain medicine experience was linked to giving injection pain treatment, while my field was pain management using pain medications. He was a completely misfit expert and obviously selected by the state because he was expected to endorse the state's findings and recommendations.

We were very skeptical that Dr. Ward's opinion was credible. He got a pain medicine certificate by fulfilling certain criteria, called "pathways," without any fellowship training. To us, he was not qualified for the job. The state's choice was not without a reason—to select a less credible expert to favor their side of the story.

We had no choice but to request another expert who had an academic background. The expert should have extensive experience in pain management and as an internist. The expert must be experienced in dealing with patients similar to our patient population, so to understand the shortcomings when dealing with such an underserved patient population, such as Medicaid. Most of our patient population for pain management were Medicaid, with limited resources. The expert who fit with these qualifications was Dr. Abraham J. Kabazie, MD. Dr. Kabazie was retained as an expert in the case. He was an MD and trained in internal medicine, and he did a fellowship in pain medicine. Dr. Kabazie had served as medical director for the Institute for Pain Medicine, Western Pennsylvania Hospital, Pittsburgh. He also served as program director for Pain Management Fellowship, Allegheny General Hospital. He held faculty positions in pain management. His research, presentations, and publications were multiple. Approximately 80 percent of his time was spent on patient care. He founded the Pittsburgh Pain Society, which is open to all Pittsburgh physicians.

CHAPTER 7

Finally, after spending thousands of hours in preparation for the hearing, the date was announced. The hearing would be in front of a hearing officer in Dover, Delaware, far from our house. Preparations were intense, with mounting tension every day. It seemed to be a moving target, with no specific focus to cover. Exploring so many dimensions required us to carry tons of files and literature. We had to hire a truck, as the files would not fit in our cars.

Losing the case could result in losing my medical license, reputation, and dignity, but I felt a sense of isolation beyond those implications. I was sure I had to fight this alone.

It was challenging to face the community and discuss changing details on a regular basis, so I kept quiet, but people often believe that silence is an acceptance of guilt. Media and newspapers ruined my reputation throughout the world. People behaved differently and avoided me, as though it was already decided that I was at fault, and that the outcome was obvious. Often, their thinking was revealed in their communication. When I attended a gathering, one person asked me, "How is your retired life going?"—assuming everything was over. Some family members constantly advised me to sell the office building to get money from it. They expected that criminal ramifications by the state would usurp the property. When I declined to sell the property, they started putting it in my wife's mind to get it done immediately, to save some money for the future. Otherwise, they said, we would lose everything.

I was also a member of a mosque committee, and people started raising voices, particularly after prayers, to release me from any mosque-related activities. This was very stressful, as the Quran clearly states how to take any news: "O you who believe! If a Fâsiq comes to you with any news, verify it, lest you should harm people in ignorance, and afterward you become regretful for what you have done" (Quran 49:6). These people considered themselves the champions of Islam but did not practice their book.

There is no such thing as privacy with the internet, and if anything is placed on Google, even if it is false, it cannot be removed. Media make information spicy and glamorous by projecting allegations. They never state that these are unproven allegations. Even if you win the case, they never go back and fix their slanderous details. They believe such changes would be detrimental to their business. There are agencies online whose business is to suppress information from a search engine like Google. Their business depends on any bad information put online and never removed or given a follow-up, such as what happened to the person against whom they projected allegations, whether the case was settled and the case's outcome, any violation of due process, and so on. So a reader is just aware of bad news, which damages the businesses and reputation. Of course, they will charge tons of money to suppress such information.

The hearing commenced before a hearing officer, relating to the two amended complaints, according to 16 Del. C. § 4734.

The hearing officer, while introducing the format of the hearing, also announced that the "burden of proof lay on the state."

The prosecutor's opening statement was outrageous. She looked angrier and more frustrated than in the first trial. With complex expressions, she seemed to add pressure and prejudice to the hearing officer, rather than directing attention to the allegations. Her opening statement was imprecise, as there was no indication of what evidence would be brought forward. With only vague commentary on the allegations, she stated that the practice was intentionally involved in egregious medical practice. I wondered if she was utterly relying on Dr. Ward to speak in her favor. She had already announced his conclusion, one month before the hearing.

The defense followed with a rebuttal opening statement, explaining that the allegations were not based on evidence but rather on perception.

After the opening remarks, proceedings formally began. As was noted in the introduction of the hearing, the prosecutor had the burden to prove allegations. She called upon the nurse practitioner to come to the witness stand. After the nurse practitioner took the oath, the prosecutor initiated a direct examination of charts and patient care. I was shocked to see that the prosecutor had brought medical charts that were arranged differently than originally submitted through subpoena. She opened a medical record and started reading through it; some sentences were highlighted, which she had marked for asking questions. The questions were fundamental, like, "What does that mean to you?" She flipped through page after page.

After many hours, she finished the questions from the first chart. The questions were random, not reflected in any specific allegations raised. It was apparent she was trying to understand medical documentation or to see if the nurse practitioner understood medical documentation. The process was prolonged and tedious. Within a day, she was not able to finish even two charts—flipping page after page with no comment on how she could prove her case. The only thing noticeable was that she tried to show the hearing officer that if she could not understand what was documented in the chart regarding patient care, then it proved gross negligence.

No investigator assisted the prosecution in this case, and no expert who had ever seen these charts was called or even mentioned. The next day was the same; the process of reading the charts continued. Day after day, the prosecution continued questioning the nurse practitioner, who was under examination for almost nine days. The prosecutor was not able to address any of the allegations that were raised, flipping charts with no clear direction.

After the nurse practitioner's testimony, the prosecutor called the state expert, Dr. Ward. The prosecutor announced that the state had approved one day for his testimony to ensure that Dr. Ward would finish his deposition by the end of the day. After the oath, the prosecutor started questioning Dr. Ward. Shockingly, her questions were mainly focused on his practice, type of service, and how he handled and treated patients with pain. Dr. Ward informed the court he was an interventional pain doctor. Describing his expertise, it was learned he was mainly a surgical interventionist to treat pain. He generally followed patients for about six months, as his approach was surgical. Subsequently, he referred patients back to their respective primary care physicians to continue care.

Dr. Ward started bragging about himself on the stand—how good he was and how carefully he examined and assessed anyone requiring pain medications. No wonder the prosecutor tried to show to the hearing officer that what Dr. Ward did in his practice was the model of "the standard of care." The inference would obviously be that any deviation of that standard would prove gross negligence. Certainly, I was concerned that this was too generic and too vague, and I was also concerned that this trick by the prosecutor would work, as the hearing officer was not a medically trained person. His only education on standard of care was the description by a single individual: Dr. Ward.

The prosecutor continued questioning. She asked a question regarding a pregnant patient who was on pain medications. "How would you handle pregnant patients on pain medications?"

Dr. Ward replied, "First, I would take the telephone and call the gyn doctor to inform him/her that the patient was taking pain medications. Then, I would wean off pain medications slowly. Reducing 10 percent per week."

His response did not include any consideration of what would happen to the patient who had severe pain. How would the doctor unilaterally decide to cut off pain medications? During pregnancy, it would be even more complicated to take a patient off pain medicines. The patient, in this case, had to accept a reduction of pain medications until entirely off pain medications. Again, the prosecutor was attempting to create a standard that most practices would not comply with. Since my practice continued pain medications during pregnancy, the prosecutor alleged that children were born addicted to pain medications, and that implied gross negligence. At this implication, I reflected that I also was a primary care doctor. I had never received a call from any pain doctor or gynecologist to be informed that the patient was taking pain medications and to stop all pain medications. The standard of care required continuing pain medications that the patient was taking before pregnancy, often noting that increasing the dosage may be needed, particularly in the second and third trimester. Even if a patient was under the treatment of a methadone clinic or on the buprenorphine treatment program, commonly during pregnancy, the mother may need more pain medications; often, the doctor has to increase pain medications.

Children are not born addicted. This is another term they were using to connote inadequate care or cruelty. The children exposed to opioids during pregnancy need to go through the withdrawal process but are not addicted. Pregnancy does not discriminate against a woman to ignore or punish her need for treatment of pain. She could have pain and other sufferings that need to be appropriately addressed. While notes were sent to obstetricians managing pregnant patients, the prosecutor spent hours discussing the expert's practice. She spent hours discussing his practice, rather than discussing the charts. This was troublesome, as she already announced that Dr. Ward was allowed only one day for his testimony.

The prosecutor then directed the questions on methadone used for pain. As she asked, "What you would do if the patient is on methadone for drug dependence and needs pain management?"

He stated he would not use methadone for such a patient for pain management, as that implied treating addiction.

The prosecutor then asked, "What do you think about patient care?"

Dr. Ward replied that he found there was "gross negligence" in care.

The prosecutor took most of the day. The time left for cross-examination was not more than an hour.

Jeff Austin, the defense attorney, finally got a chance to question. Standing at the podium, he inquired whether Dr. Ward really went through the charts and if his opinion was based on his independent study of the charts. He asked, "When did you receive the medical records?"

After a pause, Dr. Ward replied, "About a week before the hearing."

That was alarming! The state prosecutor had previously disclosed his opinion of the expert testimony approximately one month before the hearing. What was the accurate account?

"Were you able to review the records in one week?"

Dr. Ward replied, "I browsed through the chart, though [some I] reviewed also."

"When did you give your opinion for the first time to the state?"

He replied, "This morning."

This contradicted the prosecutor's statement, which in an official email, informed the defense attorney of Dr. Ward's opinion about one month before the hearing.

"Do you take Medicaid?"

He replied, "No. Medicaid pays less than the expense."

He was informed that all of the patients in the discussion were Medicaid-related. The defense continued. "Do you do pain management?"

He replied, "Since I am an interventional pain doctor, I generally follow for six months."

Mr. Austin asked, "Do you see pregnant patients in your pain clinic?"

He replied, "Two to three times in the last few years."

Mr. Austin opened the chart, which Dr. Ward claimed he had reviewed. Then, Mr. Austin went through the history, examination, review of the system, past medical history, lab, consultations, diagnostic workup, testing, and treatment, and he asked, "Do you find all these things here?" Dr. Ward agreed. It was apparent he was seeing these things for the first time. Mr. Austin asked, "Do you agree with the treatment?"

Dr. Ward nodded. "I can see there was a treatment written."

Mr. Austin opened another chart and asked Dr. Ward if he was aware that this patient also had these other problems. Dr. Ward replied that he was not aware of that. Mr. Austin continued presenting multiple consultations and informing him about the patient care given, reviewing consults from various specialists for different medical problems.

Mr. Austin opened a consultation note and read where an interventional pain doctor wrote that he agreed with the treatment plan of Dr. Niaz. Clearly, it was news to him. After reviewing a few charts with Dr. Ward, he mostly nodded in affirmation.

Then Mr. Austin asked him a question regarding a pregnant patient who was on pain medications. "What would be your approach?"

Dr. Ward replied he would have weaned her off pain medications, as they were harmful to the baby.

Mr. Austin further asked, "Can you give any referenced article to support your opinion?"

Dr. Ward replied, "I do not follow gyn literature."

Why was he was giving an expert opinion when he said he did not follow gynecological literature?

Mr. Austin asked further questions regarding the use of methadone for pain management on a patient who was taking methadone. Dr. Ward replied he would not continue methadone since methadone was used for the treatment of addiction.

Again, Mr. Austin asked, "Can you quote any medical article which supports your opinion?"

Dr. Ward replied, "I don't remember off the top of my head, but I will send you some." He never provided any such references, even after the hearing.

In fact, it is safer to use the same medications, as the conversion from methadone is extremely difficult. Methadone has an exceptionally long half-life; plus, methadone has less potential for addiction, as it gives less feeling of being "high." So, if a physician needs to convert methadone to other pain medications, like oxycodone or morphine, the dose would be enormously high, as the conversion factor with morphine to methadone could be twelve. If a patient is taking 100 mg of methadone, converting into morphine would require 1200 mg, which is enormous and probably would not be prescribed by any doctor. Generally, people who are on methadone take 120–140 mg, and some may require a much higher dose, so conversion is dangerous. It is better to use the same medication.

Opioid dosage is measured as a unit equal to morphine. This is a traditional yardstick that is used to quantify the amount of medication that is needed to convert from one narcotic to another. In conversion, it is essential to know how long the patient has been taking the medication to count tolerance in making such a decision. Generally, oxycodone is 1.5 to morphine. So, 10 mg of oxycodone is equivalent to 15 mg of morphine, in terms of dose equivalent. But when it comes to methadone, the conversion is not only enormously high but also increases with increasing dosage, which would be extremely difficult and risky to prescribe.

The standard procedure is to use methadone for pain in divided dosage. It was apparent that Dr. Ward's knowledge regarding the practical application of pain medications was superficial. He was unaware of problems facing a primary care physician when a patient needed pain medications with multiple comorbid conditions. He was there to endorse the allegations of the state. In doing so, he did not realize that he was recommending malpractice.

Mr. Austin asked him for the interpretation of urine toxicology. "What would you do if a patient on pain medication has urine toxicology positive with cocaine?"

Dr. Ward replied,

> And if they test positive for cocaine, then they're a substance abuser. They've probably been a substance abuser. They've probably been a substance abuser their whole life, and they still continue to be a substance abuser. And that patient certainly is not going to get any controlled substances from me. Now, if they have a contracture, or I need to write them a splint, they're—like okay, you have a drug problem. I'm never going to write you a CDS. However, I'll tell you what can be done to help you, and I'll refer you to an addiction place. But it helps them to be honest with me. The people that I have the least tolerance with are the people that look me in the eye and lie to me, and then I catch them lying to me. You know, I'm usually going to get rid of them. I don't have—you know, if you don't have an honest relationship, then I really am not in a position to help them.

Urine toxicology is part of the workup that helps a doctor to understand a patient. It is not a tool used to justify or discharge a patient. The Federation of State Medical Boards published a book 2008, *Responsible Opioid Prescribing*. Written in the second edition on page 81: "If this testing is employed, as in all therapeutic decisions, it must be used solely in the service of the patient's best interest."

Urine toxicologies do not guide one direction. There was an article written in *Topics in Pain Management* 25, no. 4 (November 2009): 1–6. Essentially, the purpose of urine toxicology is to provide better care to a patient. Based on urine toxicology, a prudent physician develops a differential diagnosis.

The question on urine toxicology to Dr. Ward was a general question, without any specific patient mentioned. This was to determine whether he understood how to interpret urine toxicology results and make a differential diagnosis and determine a line of action based on scientific information. He should first inquire whether the test was done at a doctor's office (screening test) or was the confirmatory test result. Tests for urine toxicology are divided into preliminary and confirmatory analyses. Preliminary tests using the immunoassay technique get quicker results but carry a risk of cross-sensitivity, resulting in a false positive or negative with other substances. In this specific question regarding cocaine positive, it could be due to a false positive so he was expected to explain the possible reasons for a test; for example, coca tea consumption could cause a positive cocaine urine test at the preliminary level. His statement clearly exposed that he was biased (SS Mazor et al., "Coca tea consumption causes positive urine cocaine assay," *Eur J Emerg Med.* 13, no. 6 (2006): 340–341).

It was clear he did not know how to interpret urine toxicology results and was there only to concur with the prosecutor's allegation. Out of frustration, he showed anger to impress the hearing officer. It was disgraceful for a professional physician on the witness stand as an expert to use street language or what one might describe as a gangster-like approach. He most likely did not realize the degree to which his descriptions could be defined as malpractice. It was clear that he did not know pain management or internal medicine.

Mr. Austin then asked, "Dr. Ward, do you have a log of time spent in reviewing these charts?"

He replied, "No."

This was important, as he was paid $500 per hour. If he did not have any log of time, then the defense was confident that he never reviewed any charts. It was blatantly obvious. He was paid to stand in the court to say my practice was doing gross negligence, yet in doing so, he failed to find any supporting article to back up his statements. The state never disclosed how much money he was paid. The only information revealed was that "he was paid $500 per hour door to door and did not include traveling expenses." Ms. Hilda, the paralegal to Mr. Austin, indicated that as the state did not pay for a hotel stay, the prosecutor paid for his stay.

The prosecutor did not let the defense continue questioning, as there was limited time, so at that point, the cross-examination had to be stopped.

CHAPTER 8

Dr. Abraham Kabazie, MD, a fellow in pain medicine, was called to the witness stand. After the oath, his testimony began. Mr. Austin went through all the charts where Dr. Ward had given an opinion in his testimony, and Dr. Kabazie answered all the questions or allegations that were raised.

We indicated we would ask and discuss allegations as long as the prosecutor wished, without time limits. Dr. Kabazie's testimony continued for over two days. Despite his busy schedule, he sacrificed his time from work to give complete testimony.

Mr. Austin asked him about the documentation. Dr. Kabazie conceded that he found glitches in the documentation. It was his opinion that the errors in the documentation did not affect the patient's health care.

Dr. Kabazie commented on the use of methadone for pain for a patient coming from the methadone clinic. He agreed that giving methadone would be better than any other narcotic pain medication used in those circumstances. He explained in detail why methadone was preferable—the conversion was difficult, and it did not give the same "high." He referred to some articles on this subject. Mr. Austin explained that the patient was not going to two places at the same time.

Mr. Austin asked about a pregnant patient who was on pain medications. Dr. Kabazie agreed he would continue pain medications, as stopping pain medication for a pregnant patient would be more harmful. When Mr. Austin said that Dr. Ward indicated he would wean pain medications off from pregnant patients, Dr. Kabazie replied that would be "malpractice." Dr. Kabazie discussed medical charts in detail that Dr. Ward was expected to review, and it was clear that Dr. Kabazie had explored these charts very well.

The prosecutor, representing the Office of the Attorney General, should be a justice model. Winning the case would make headlines in the newspaper but could result in the loss of dignity and in the people's confidence, without a standard of professionalism or accuracy. The prosecutor, however, explored the charts with Dr. Kabazie in an attempt to dig out something to support her allegations. Dr. Kabazie obviously could not stay in the courtroom for an extended period, so part of his testimony was through video conference from his hometown in Pennsylvania. Of the sixty claims raised by the prosecutor, Dr. Kabazie's testimony did not support even one of the allegations. But it appeared the witch hunt would continue.

The nurse practitioner testified for nine days, so I expected my testimony to be as long. The prosecutor called me to the witness box. After the oath, the prosecutor placed a chart in front of me and asked me to review the medical record. While I was going through the medical record, the prosecutor asked, "Is this one of your patients?"

"Yes, one of the patients from my office."

"Does the chart belong to that patient?"

I replied, "Yes."

The same process repeated multiple times; she was only trying to confirm if the charts belonged to these patients. No question related to any documentation or patient care was asked. I could not understand what she was up to or how she was trying to prove anything inside the chart, just by asking if that chart belonged to me or not.

I did not realize at that time that the underlying strategy was to use the hearing officer as an expert, even though he had no medical background or experience. The prosecutor presented charts to the hearing officer to review on his own, and the procedure was to ascertain that the medical records were authentically linked to my care, just to satisfy the law. I did not think about the underlying strategy, or I would have reviewed the charts in greater detail to verify the information was not missed. I discovered this strategy later on, when I read the description from the hearing officer in his document, "Facts and Findings," which we would discuss later on.

He claimed the practice did not submit paper charts, and only electronic medical records were presented. As previously described, medical records were divided into two parts—review of symptoms, physical examination, medications listing, ICD 9, and part of the treatment was kept in the computer as an electronic chart, and the rest were followed in the paper folder as a paper chart. In reality, paper records were the actual working chart.

This was another hideous tactic to win the case. Another loophole in the law that, sadly and unfairly, impacts justice.

After providing charts to the hearing officer, the prosecutor opened information from the *Physicians' Desk Reference* (PDR) and loudly read the side effects of one of the pain medications, word by word, line by line. Many of the side effects mentioned in the PDR were only found in animal studies and might never occur in human beings, but they have to write them in the PDR for information purposes. After going through these side effects, she asked me if I had discussed all these side effects with the patient before prescribing pain medication.

I informed her that if she would look at my pain contract, she would see that it mentions most of the common side effects in human beings, and the patient has to sign it. She got irritated, announcing that these were just the forms that were thrown to a patient to sign, implying that those patients did not understand what they were signing and that I had not discussed it with them. She emphasized that those things should not be counted as information given to the patient.

I indicated that the information she was reading from the PDR was for informative purposes, not for a regulatory sense. The PDR is not the standard of care. She then closed the PDR. She changed the subject and pulled out the model policy. She started reading elements of the model policy to reflect that the medical notes were not written according to these headings, so there was egress from the standard of care. Again, I indicated that the model policy regarding documentation is good but yet not regulatory. In fact, the book that accompanies the model policy, *Responsible Opioid Prescribing* by Dr. Scott Fishman, itself indicated that "most doctors do not write medical notes on the model policy. in fact, many doctors are not even aware of the model policy." Since I agreed that the model policy regarding documentation was good, she projected that statement as acceptance of guilt. She took on the characteristics of an expert when she said that the documentation should have been written on that pattern. She expected that the hearing officer would agree with her.

Subsequently, she changed the subject and started questioning the nurse practitioner to show the hearing officer that my supervision was weak, ignoring the fact that the nurse practitioner carried her own independent authority; my agreement with her was to provide consultations. She asked whether the nurse practitioner was qualified to practice pain management. Again, I indicated that the criteria are determined by the regulatory organizations that issue her medical license and controlled substance registration. Nurse practitioners have an independent prescriptive authority, certified by the licensing board, and that was required as a qualification to prescribe pain medication. It was not at my prerogative, as the collaborating physician.

No wonder my testimony was short and ended quickly. I expected that she would discuss allegations, as the burden of proof rested on the prosecutor, but no charges were presented or discussed with me.

After her questioning, Mr. Austin went through all the charts that were related to my patients' medical care and on which Dr. Ward had commented. He went through charts in detail and asked questions related to patient care. The prosecutor had the opportunity to cross-question, but she declined.

I thought the prosecutor would discuss with me the interpretation of urine toxicology. Surprisingly, she did not raise any questions related to urine toxicology. This subject was touched on briefly by both experts, Dr. Kabazie and Dr. Ward, who agreed that interpreting drug screening tests, even by an expert, "is a challenge and requires an understanding of opiate drug metabolism, pharmacokinetics, and limits of laboratory testing methods."

The defense presented multiple pieces of literature, with both the experts agreeing with the content. When literature was presented to Dr. Ward regarding the interpretation of urine toxicology, he also agreed with the author of that article, that "clinicians should consider a differential diagnosis for abnormal urine drug screen results, including drug abuse, addictions, self-treatment, a poorly controlled pain, psychological issues, or diversion." The relevancy of these articles, according to Dr. Kabazie's testimony, was that if a patient tests negative for a particular drug, it may be because of his metabolism or that he is *undertreated* for pain and is taking more than prescribed, which is what is meant by *pseudoaddiction.* Dr. Kabazie specifically testified that "undertreatment can result in pain, which can be treated by *increasing* medications."

Another subject where this case initially rested was overprescribing narcotic pain medications. Both experts agreed that "there is no upper limit of opioids, as a rule." In fact, this is where the terms *opioid-tolerant* and *opioid-naive* come into play. Overprescription is not a number of prescriptions that a prescriber crosses; rather, it requires examining the patient to determine its effects by examining patients as to how a medication affects their daily health, including breathing, performing daily and gainful activities, and reducing the patients' suffering. It is also imperative to see other circumstances and comorbid conditions. A terminally ill patient does need to treat pain aggressively. A patient must be examined before it can be concluded that the provider is overprescribing. Also, it is vital to monitor medicine diversion or misuse. These issues, I thought, would be part of the discussion. I did not have any idea how the prosecutor could reach such conclusions without an in-depth cross-examination. It was the reliance on perception that subsequently confirmed to me that this was a witch hunt.

It was time for the closing remarks. Almost eleven days had already passed. It would obviously become more economically burdensome to continue. We wanted to have a quick closing discussion. The hearing officer also wanted a concise closing discussion, as all the evidence should have already been presented. The closing arguments were merely to highlight the strong points for both parties and rest the discussion. The hearing officer said he wanted to finish the closing arguments in a day.

The prosecutor commenced with the closing argument. Instead of going through the evidence presented in the trial, she started a new conversation. She pulled urine toxicology results from a few charts and indicated that the practice was ignoring clear evidence of drug abuse or diversion. She based her allegations on positive or negative urine toxicology results. She said that if the urine toxicology result was negative, that was clear evidence that the practice ignored this very evidence of diversion so egress from the standard of care, as she stated, "ignoring the unmistakable sign of drug abuse and diversion." She picked the results randomly; it was like shooting blindly in the dark. Out of context, the information she highlighted might seem like negligence. It was like taking a few lines from a textbook and manipulating them to prove something. She did this, even though the experts had discussed earlier at this trial that the interpretation of urine toxicology is complicated.

Further, she took the entire day for her closing arguments. The hearing officer requested ending the closing arguments within a day, but the time left for our response after she finished was not more than an hour. We had no choice but to ask the hearing officer to extend for another day.

Our goal was to bring forward the urine toxicology results, which the prosecutor claimed showed negligence. Fortunately, this was on a Friday, so we had a couple of days to go through the charts. We spent the weekend on this task. Jeff decided to project the urine toxicology results on placards so that everyone in the room could view them easily and could ask questions. We began our closing argument, emphasizing that the burden of proof rested with the prosecutor and that she had failed to prove any of the allegations. Shockingly, the prosecutor came with a tablet and continuously played with it while the defense presented the closing argument. This was very insulting and showed her arrogance, disapproval, and lack of professional concern for all parties in the case. There almost seemed to be a feeling of hatred in her demeanor.

The urine toxicology results were presented on placards. We were proving that the urine toxicology results, which the prosecutor showed were negative, had their metabolites positive in the same urine toxicology tests. However, she could not understand this complex analysis.

Most of the drug goes through a process of breaking down, and by-products are known as *metabolites*. The presence of metabolites indicates the patient is taking the medication chronically. Some patients are fast metabolizers, so their medications metabolize much quicker than others, and their metabolites are visible much earlier. These metabolites have different chemical names. A person not trained in toxicology might think the prescribed medication was absent, and the illicit drug was positive, but in reality, it is positive based on metabolites.

As we were presenting this critical evidence, which could possibly aid the prosecutor in future prosecution, she paid no attention and continued reading on her tablet. I reflected that she either was greatly confident that whatever we produced as evidence would not change the outcome of the litigation, or she was very arrogant. Throughout the litigation process, she was very prejudiced, using phrases that showed disrespect; for example, she had commented on the documentation as "garbage in, garbage out." Again, not the professionalism I expected to encounter in serious judicial proceedings.

Our closing argument was mainly a rebuttal of what she had presented earlier in the case. We were relaxed, as the prolonged battle finally was ending. We were confident the result would go in our favor. We were optimistic that there would be professionals with a medical background in the deliberation, who would examine the evidence honestly, thoroughly, and professionally; with their expertise, we felt they would agree with us.

After an exasperating two weeks, we now had to wait for the deliberation. Jeff invited me for dinner. There was a restaurant in Dover, Delaware, near the lake, and we all agreed to go there. It was a relaxing evening; after all, we were tired and stressed, even panicky at times because of the fear of the unknown. I believe any litigation process is burdensome, even if a person is confident of winning. Justice was expected by those who were not present in person, and they had to rely on the information presented in the hearing, mainly the "Facts and Findings" by the hearing officer.

I still had one significant concern in my mind: the persons in the deliberation were professional but still volunteers. The time required to go through all the documents in detail before concluding justice would be enormous and demanding. After all, they had their primary responsibilities at their jobs, and taking time out from work would be difficult. At that point, however, there was nothing we could do except wait and pray.

CHAPTER 9

After the hearing, we were confident, as the state had failed to produce evidence supporting the allegations. My attorney and I were hopeful that the hearing officer would write his findings and assessment, acknowledging that fact.

The hearing officer took a few months to write "Facts and Findings" and recommendations, based on his assessment, according to the law. This produced a 240-page document that explained the litigation process and the outcome, based on his assessment. The documentation was sent to the Delaware Medical Licensing Board to proceed with the deliberation on this case. A copy was also sent to us.

When we reviewed the document written by the hearing officer, we realized he had written of things not even mentioned by the prosecutor. During the hearing, I was suspicious that the prosecutor gave charts to the hearing officer without discussing any allegation, essentially transferring the prosecution's responsibility to the hearing officer. My suspicion was correct, as "Facts and Findings" by the hearing officer was clearly a prosecution without the need to involve defense—prosecutorial misconduct. It was a one-sided story, and since he was not a medically trained person, we noticed multiple errors in the descriptions and assessment. The hearing officer's findings were devastating and were intended to prove most of the allegations raised by the state. Findings were based on his own study of the charts. His lack of practical knowledge of medicine was clearly noticeable. We had to write exceptions to the "Facts and Findings." We had one concern—that the Deliberation Committee would naturally assume that the hearing officer was neutral and would lean on his side.

It was very technical and tedious work. We had to write exceptions backed by the references, as the defense provided during the hearing. It would produce a very lengthy report, which would not be possible for members of the Deliberation Committee—a group of volunteers—to thoroughly study before reaching a conclusion. Still, we ended up writing a report that was almost 150 pages long and mentioned only significant errors by the hearing officer, titled "Exceptions to the Facts and Findings."

Why had the hearing officer announced at the start of the hearing that the burden of proof lay on the state? That implied that the role of the defense was to rebut any evidence presented by the prosecutor and cross-examine any evidence or findings presented at the hearing. The prosecutor mainly went through medical records with the nurse practitioner, flipping page after page, with no reference to any allegation. The prosecutor presented no significant evidence. The only evidence presented was the testimony of Dr. William Ward, which was strongly rebutted by Dr. Kabazie.

The chief hearing officer did acknowledge, however, that "pursuant to a collaborative agreement between N. P. [nurse practitioner] and Dr. Niaz, the Nurse Practitioner was *lawfully* authorized to exercise *independent authority* to prescribe controlled substances for patients of Tri-State." He also recognized that, based on the evidence presented, that N. P. had the legal right to do so until her authority was curtailed by Dr. Niaz.

The prosecutor then twisted things around in the next statement by saying the nurse practitioner was an employee of Tri-State and that I had the "professional obligation and duty to supervise her." She did agree that "Dr. Niaz met with her on a regular weekly basis to discuss patient care and other issues. Dr. Niaz (or a temporary substitute during his absences) was always available to Nurse Practitioner Binkley to give input, guidance, and supervision as needed." The prosecutor totally ignored the key concept with regard to an independent prescriber, like a nurse practitioner: whether and when adequate supervision is required, considering her credentials, which of course affords her more independence than a med-tech or an RN. The law regulating the relationship between collaborating physician and advanced nurse practitioner is mentioned in Delaware laws:

27.2.1 Submit a copy of the current collaborative agreement to the Joint Practice Committee (JPC). The collaborative agreement(s) shall include arrangements for consultation and/or referral and/or hospitalization complementary to the area of the nurse's independent Practice.

The hearing officer completely ignored the laws of the state. Not a word is mentioned in the requirement for an advanced nurse practitioner with independent prescriptive authority to be supervised by a physician. Supervision is required to those nonphysicians working in the office, like med-tech, a front desk person, or other persons working to help a provider in the office. The law clearly states that the relationship is for a consultation, so if the nurse practitioner needs advice or consultation in managing a complicated case, then he/she should have access. There was no evidence that any nurse practitioner was denied such access or discussion.

As written in the "Exceptions":

This was totally contradictory to what was presented in the Hearing. She was working as an Independent Contractor since she had a Collaborative Agreement with Dr. Niaz, so she was provided with guidelines and instructions as part of the agreement.

The Internal Revenue Service defines an *independent contractor* as follows:

An individual is an independent contractor if the payer has the right to control or direct only the result of the work and not what will be done and how it will be done. The earnings of a person who is working as an independent contractor are subject to Self-Employment Tax.

That definition certainly suggests it was an error that the NP was not an independent contractor. Even if one hires a contractor to build a house or perform any service, specific guidelines have to be given, quality of work evaluated, and review of the material used. Still, these inputs do not make such a person an employee. The chief hearing officer was holding me responsible for whatever deficiencies he found in the nurse practitioner's treatment of her patients, even though under regulations in Delaware, these employees are independent practitioners. The whole argument was nonsense. Whether she was a contractor or an employee did not make any difference. She had independent prescriptive authority, and that authority, by law, did not need supervision. I was unjustifiably held responsible for the nurse practitioner's actions.

The prosecution wrote that I had the "professional obligation and duty to supervise her." What was inappropriately discounted was that she was working on a contract basis, and the fact that she was paid as a contractor, carrying her own professional liability, was ignored. Further, the hearing officer stated that the nurse practitioner was prescribing phentermine incorrectly. In his "Facts and Findings," he referred to the fact that on at least one occasion, the nurse practitioner prescribed phentermine for a patient without checking authoritative texts for information on whether the drug was contraindicative. This apparently was based on information in the *Physicians' Desk Reference* (PDR), ignoring again that the PDR does not dictate the standard of care. Furthermore, whether it was appropriate to prescribe phentermine must be based on expert testimony, after considering all of the patient's personal circumstances. There was no expert testimony offered as to whether it was appropriate or inappropriate to prescribe phentermine to the patient involved.

In the exceptions for the licensing board to consider before deliberating on this case:

> It was explicitly recognized by the Chief Hearing Officer that he would not only meet with her weekly to discuss patient care, he also had an "open door" policy. He remained available to advise her and provide guidance at all other times. The only other Nurse Practitioner from Dr. Niaz's Practice to testify was Michelle Lewis, A.P.N, whose hearing testimony was taken at the time of January 25, 2012, Controlled Substance Advisor Committee and entered into evidence at this Hearing. When asked by the State what training she was provided by Dr. Niaz,

Nurse Practitioner Lewis testified that when she went to work for Tri-State, Dr. Niaz discussed with her what he expected of her. Dr. Niaz told her and showed what he expected as it was related to prescribing pain medications and primary care. Nurse Practitioner Lewis also testified that she would talk to Dr. Niaz every day and meet with him on Fridays for a minimum of an hour. During the Friday meetings, Nurse Practitioner Lewis testified that most of the discussions concentrated on pain management patients because they were the "difficult ones, the ones that I didn't want to prescribe to, or were in question about." The amount of time and attention Dr. Niaz spent with the Nurse Practitioners at Tri-State, despite each having independent prescriptive authority, appears to have been given little consideration by the Chief Hearing Officer in making his Recommendation in this case. However, what does not appear to be given weight by the Chief Hearing Officer was the fact that, solely as a result of the concerns of a Newark pharmacist which was subsequently invalidated, Dr. Niaz on his own made the decision to suspended Nurse Practitioner's authority to write controlled substances while employed in his office as of 7/15/11. Within the agreement, he would review all of her patient files and directly evaluate the patients with her as well.

Why did the hearing officer not consider this fact? What was the purpose? I still believed the allegation was a witch hunt. With the public sensitivity to the growing concern of opioid misuse, the state intended to make an example of me and show that they were combating the opioid crisis and supporting the benefits of their new prescription monitoring program.

There was an assertion that the practice provided incomplete medical records. The hearing officer concluded erroneously that the practice only sent the electronic version of the medical records. He wrote:

> The records which Dr. Niaz chose to provide to the state pursuant to its subpoenas duces tecum and other "discovery" requests were largely printouts of the electronically maintained files. ... Dr. Niaz chose the system he would use and decided how to present patient charts to the state prior to January 2012. ... Dr. Niaz's counsel argued that his client tried his best to explain the charts to a state investigator.

Nor was the investigator presented as evidence, neither did the prosecutor raise this allegation; how the hearing officer concluded was a clear example of his biased approach.

The hearing officer, acting as a medically trained expert, was not able to differentiate between paper and computer records. Paper records simply mean records kept in the paper folder for patient care. The EMR had other information that might look redundant, as some of the information was brought forward from prior visits. It was clearly explained during the hearing that all those deficiencies were corrected and never affected patient care, as the expert, Dr. Kabazie, also testified.

One is reminded in this statement of the reliability of using only an assumption. Records were provided on the spot when Mr. Brady brought the subpoena to the office. The practice copied and gave all the charts to him immediately while he was sitting in the office. There were so many papers that anyone, particularly nonmedical persons, would be confused. I expected that they would call me to discuss these charts, but they never called me, and even in the hearing, they did not want to talk about any chart with me. In printing out records from the EMR, the staff provided documents in every possible way.

The most important issue was the impact this had on patient care. On that important issue, Dr. Kabazie testified that, as it related to the five files specifically referred by the state's expert, Dr. Ward, involving actual treatment by Dr. Niaz, "it did not prevent Dr. Niaz from meeting the standard of care relating to the treatment these five patients received."

Though the hearing officer thought overprescription would be the central theme of the case, the prosecutor did not bother to bring this issue. This was the primary allegation that sparked the investigation; in other words, the eye of the storm. The perception the state wanted to instigate was that the practice had overly prescribed pain medications.

The key point ignored was the letter written by the vice president of the Union Hospital, explaining and clarifying that a large bulk of pain management patients were recently accepted only at his request. The statement did not receive the merit it deserved. In the "Exceptions," we wrote,

> It is respectfully submitted that a mitigating factor in this case in favor of Dr. Niaz should be that the Chief Hearing Officer recognized that Dr. Niaz agreed to accept "as many" of Dr. Shah's patients "as he could accommodate" and to a lesser extent he did the same as it related to Dr. Cooper's patients. There was a specific finding of fact that the chief motivating factor for Dr. Niaz to have agreed to this was his concern to do what was in these patients' best interest: The diversion (drug diversion is a medical and legal concept involving the transfer of any legally prescribed controlled substances from the individual for whom it was prescribed to another person for any illicit use). However, it is respectfully submitted that the actual testimony was that these techniques were not only utilized to detect diversion but also to maximize patient compliance with the medication they were taking relating to patient care issues.

We also presented the procedure and monitoring protocols utilized in the practice to the relevant parties, particularly for compliance and diversion. In fact, the hearing officer also highlighted multiple techniques used by my practice to detect drug abuse and to provide continuity of care. Specifically, after hearing the testimony, the chief hearing officer noted that he accepted my testimony that I made the decision to take on the new patients from Dr. Shah's and Dr. Cooper's practices to help other physicians and to accommodate pain patients who required a continuity of care and medication. In fact, the chief hearing officer specifically noted that he accepted my testimony that I "was primarily motivated by a concern for patient health and safety in doing so." Dr. Kabazie also recognized that I was attempting to treat pain with available medications, which was often tricky because Medicaid restricted formulary.

Dr. Ward testified related to the care of a patient, James Sr. "Specifically, he gave his opinion about writing pain medications when the patient had emphysema." Dr. Ward's opinion was that the amount of pain medication would be totally unreasonable for this patient because he had emphysema and was on oxygen, and this would suppress his respiratory drive. Dr. Ward offered that opinion, even though it is accepted in the specialty of pain management that there are no upper limits on the amount of opioid medication that can be prescribed, and even though James Sr. was a prime example of a patient who would be considered "opiate-tolerant."

Also, and incredibly significant, during cross-examination, it became clear that when Dr. Ward gave his opinion on James Sr. for the first time on the morning of the hearing, he did not even know that the patient James Sr. was seen on multiple occasions by a cardiothoracic surgeon, by a cardiologist, and by a pulmonologist or that there were any of those specialists' records in the file. In fact, it was only during cross-examination that he was shown proof—from the very file to which he had testified he reviewed in order to give an opinion—that James Sr. was "well-known to the cardiothoracic surgery service." Moreover, in offering an opinion on the appropriateness of the amount of pain medication James Sr. received, Dr. Ward admitted that he did not know any of the details relating to the pulmonary surgery that James Sr. had undergone, which was a wedge resection of his lung. When asked whether he agreed that a wedge resection was one of the most painful surgeries a person can undergo, he testified that he did not necessarily agree with that, but he was willing to concede that "your ribs are a pain generator" and that "when you put in chest tubes or anything else, it is painful."

In fact, as the chief hearing officer correctly recognized in the recommendation, "the State is no longer alleging that the scripts presented to Ms. Krause (the Newark pharmacist) represented 'overprescribing' or other evidence of unprofessional conduct per se in this case." This statement in the recommendation should have been the emphasis of the hearing. This was a huge point. It was my rationale for telling this cautionary tale and the source of my anguish and frustration. The state basically stated that there was no longer a case, as they were no longer alleging that the prescriptions represented overprescribing. Instead of resting their case at this juncture, they looked to their own personal agenda—to introduce additional allegations in order to make me the example, advance their program, and not lose the case.

The chief hearing officer agreed that despite this "concern," the state failed to prove that any excess prescriptions were written by the nurse practitioner or any other provider at Tri-State. The hearing officer rested much of his opinion on the testimony of Dr. Ward. In fact, he mentioned him as an internist and pain medicine specialist.

Another critical difference in Dr. Ward's practice was the undisputed fact that, unlike me, he did *not* accept Medicaid as either a primary or secondary insurer. This was obviously a critical difference since the state presented him as an expert to pass judgment, but he not only treated patients for an average of six months total but did not accept the very type of insurance that I accepted for 50 percent or more of my patient population, even though I know that patients on Medicaid often have limited treatment options.

We mentioned in our "Exceptions of the Facts and Findings" a very important point to note to evaluate the reasonableness of the weight that the chief hearing officer has given Dr. Ward's testimony. It is undisputed that contrary to the conclusions reached in his recommendation, Dr. Ward admitted that he received all twenty-seven of the patient files from the state a week or less before he testified at the hearing on June 15, 2012. It's equally as compelling that this was after the state answered expert interrogatories on May 24, 2012, indicating that Dr. Ward was expected to testify that the "respondents were unprofessional in their care."

It is crystal clear and also compelling that, based on the sworn testimony of Dr. Ward, he had not even received the records, let alone reviewed them, at the time the state represented what his opinions would be at the hearing. Accordingly, especially in light of everything else that he admitted at the hearing, this shows how biased and/or predetermined his expert testimony was going to be in this case. Even the hearing officer noticed changes in opinion by Dr. Ward as an expert. As the chief hearing officer correctly noted, Dr. Ward clarified his opinion (albeit only when forced to do so during cross-examination) that Dr. Niaz and Nurse Practitioner Binkley "did much correctly."

Most disturbing because of what was at stake in this case, he admitted that he only "browsed" through the twenty-seven files. Knowing he would be paid for his file review, it is also telling that when asked specifically how much time he spent reviewing the files prior to the morning of the hearing, Dr. Ward testified that he was *not* planning to bill for the time he spent preparing (despite estimating that it was a lot of hours) and that he had not even kept track of the amount of time spent. It cannot be emphasized enough—the opinions he offered at the hearing were given to the state for the first time that morning.

Dr. Kabazie testified, based on his practice alone. He was in a far better position to testify as an expert in this case than Dr. Ward. Thirty percent of Dr. Kabazie's patients are on Medicaid or eligible under a Pennsylvania public assistance program. One percent of Dr. Kabazie's patient population must pay cash for services. Dr. Kabazie also specifically addressed the second issue raised by Dr. Ward, which was the appropriate treatment of pregnant pain-management patients who were already on opioid pain medications. It specifically related to the appropriate treatment of pregnant patients at Tri-State. Patients, who were counseled about the problems associated with getting pregnant while on pain medications, had a specific provision contained in the pain management contract that each patient was required to sign. Dr. Kabazie made it clear that it was dangerous to reduce or, in most cases, change the medications of those patients. In fact, Dr. Kabazie specifically gave the opinion that Dr. Ward's opinion on this issue, *if implemented*, would constitute "malpractice."

CHAPTER 10

Another conclusion of the hearing officer was the reference to the practice's treating addiction rather than pain. The chief hearing officer specifically found a valid point made by Dr. Ward regarding the practice of Tri-State on more than one occasion, prescribing pain medication in the form of methadone for a patient who was receiving the same medication for drug addiction. This conclusion was drawn on inaccurate interpretations. The hearing officer concluded that it appeared as if the patient was going to two places simultaneously. This was totally erroneous, and I could not imagine that a person with a background in law could make such a blunder. It was intentional, putting fuel on the fire to win the case, as no evidence was presented to support this conclusion.

To do exactly what Dr. Ward claimed was "professionally irresponsible," as pointed out at the hearing, was permissible under federal law. Dr. Kabazie, who testified on my behalf, did address this very point. In fact, Dr. Kabazie specifically testified that not only was it appropriate to prescribe methadone for a patient who was getting the same drug for heroin addiction, but it would be "the drug of choice" for such a patient who had been on that drug for an extended period because he/she would not get the "euphoria" that would be present with other types of opioids. The chief hearing officer suggested that when it became necessary to medicate such a patient with oxycodone for breakthrough pain, I should have brought the patient in daily to monitor his/her drug use. This was contrary to Dr. Kabazie's specific testimony.

There should have been discussion in the hearing to conclude why these patients were receiving pain medications and ended up in my practice, but that was not asked. I had volunteered to treat hepatitis C infection for patients coming to Brandywine Drug Rehab Center without any fees. Some of these patients did not have insurance, or their insurance did not cover hepatitis C treatment. I realized that many patients coming to the methadone clinic had multiple comorbid conditions. Many patients had only one option for receiving pain medication for their underlying painful conditions. This was to admit that they had an addiction and therefore would be qualified to receive methadone, a highly effective pain medication. Generally, this happened when their pain-management doctor refused to continue pain medications. Some such patients who had hepatitis C accompanied with comorbid pain pathology were accepted to my office for further management.

At that time, treatment for hepatitis C was a combination of interferon with ribavirin. The treatment was lengthy and complicated, requiring close monitoring. I decided to continue treating their painful conditions with methadone. They were never allowed to take this treatment or drug simultaneously from both places. As written in "Exceptions to the Facts and Findings":

> No patient was given Methadone for the Pain who at the same time was also being treated for drug addiction at a Methadone clinic. For reasons already set forth herein, there was no evidence presented by the State that Dr. Niaz or anyone else at Tri-state ever prescribed Methadone while the patient was simultaneously securing daily dosages from (presumably Methadone) clinics as noted by the Chief Hearing Officer on the Recommendation. Rather, the evidence presented by the respondents showed just the opposite. These patients were accepted not to treat just for pain, but for Hepatitis C treatment and other medical issues.

The hearing officer also concluded that prescribing pain medication to a patient whose urine was positive with heroin was a violation of the care standard. The hearing officer wrote, "Dr. Ward testified that because James Jr. had used heroin, it is not standard of care to treat him because he is an active heroin user"; even though Dr. Kabazie opined, "Not only is it within the clinical judgment of Dr. Niaz to have treated the patient under these circumstances but based on his thorough review of the file, Dr. Niaz's decision to do so was within the standard of care." Again, the assertion bears repeating. It is imperative to always have an expert who is qualified with an appropriate academic background to give an opinion in a court.

Often, physicians direct their course of action solely on the interpretation of urine toxicology results, which may be very misleading, and discharge patients from the practice inappropriately. The fear among health care providers is that if the regulatory authorities see the urine toxicology results, they will suspend their licenses.

For example, a term used in pain management is *pseudoaddiction*. A patient may appear addicted and have addictive behavior but is not addicted. Pseudoaddiction (*pseudo* from Latin, meaning "fake, not real") was originally introduced and defined by Weissman and Haddox in 1989, as an "iatrogenic syndrome that mimics the behavioral symptoms of addiction" in patients receiving inadequate doses of opioids for pain (DE Weissman and JD Haddox, "Opioid pseudo addiction—an iatrogenic syndrome, *Pain* 36, no. 3 (1989):363–6, doi 10.1016/0304-3959(89)90097-3). Weissman and Haddox proposed that patients who present with pseudoaddiction go through three phases: stimulus, escalation, and crisis. In stimulus, at pain onset, the patient receives inadequate analgesia and requests more medication, frequently requesting specific drugs by name. In escalation, the patient realizes that to obtain an additional prescription, he or she has to convince a health care provider of the legitimacy of his or her pain. In the crisis phase, culminating when unrelieved pain continues, the patient engages in increasingly bizarre drug-seeking behaviors, leading to "a crisis of mistrust," with anger and isolation by the patient and frustration and avoidance by the health care team.

When commenting on urine toxicology results in the documentation, the hearing officer, in his "conclusions of law," found that the state, in part, had proven the allegation that I "prescribed controlled substances without taking reasonable and necessary precautions to prevent illegal diversion." It further stated, by accepting inferences without any expert testimony, that "the tox screens performed by Tri-State and by Ameritox *occasionally* produced evidence of the use of illegal drugs." At other times, they established that Tri-State patients were taking medications I had not prescribed and still other instances of absence of medications that were prescribed.

The hearing officer's decision to interpret urine toxicology results on his own was unprofessional. This was driven by the closing arguments as the prosecutor brought forward—for the first time—results of some of the urine toxicologies. These results were never discussed by the experts. There was a specific finding of fact by the hearing officer that some of the patients at Tri-State would go months without being subjected to toxicology screens or, in the alternative, were only subjected to the less-reliable point-of-care testing. It was a clinical decision never discussed in the hearing, without noting a specific standard of care of how many times a provider should perform a urine toxicology.

Still, we rebutted her findings when she introduced urine toxicology results. The finding was based on reading positive and negative results on spot urine toxicology reports. Despite multiple pieces of literature submitted during the hearing, the hearing officer completely ignored that both Dr. Ward and Dr. Kabazie avoided interpretation of urine toxicology in any specific patient care.

Urine toxicology is done to know more about a patient and not just to punish the patient. Ameritox was a company that provided physicians with urine drug monitoring and reporting services. Ameritox published a study that was introduced into evidence; in a retrospective analysis of nearly one million urine drug testing results from chronic pain patients across the country, it found that "as many as 75% of the patients were not taking their medications as prescribed: Some were taking less, others were taking more, and some were taking additional prescription medications their pain doctors didn't know about."

Nonetheless, Ameritox concluded that these abnormal tests do not mean that all are misusing or abusing drugs. Instead, the conclusion was that the drug test might simply mean that "something" has gone wrong and that it is enough that the physician speaks to the patient to look further into what issue there might be.

As stated in an article from *Topics in Pain Management* 25, no. 4 (Nov. 2009): 6–9, both positive and negative results carry a differential diagnosis. Initial urine toxicology screens, based on immunoassay screens, are qualitative tests with positive and negative findings. A negative has a cutoff number. For example, opiates generally have a cutoff number of 300 ng/mL. This means if the opiate is less than 300 ng per milliliter in the urine, then the test result is negative. A medication may be present in the urine but below the detectable level. This cutoff is necessary because for every test procedure, there is a method of "validation," which validates test results. Even in the range where the test is read as positive or negative, there is a need to know about the "sensitivity" and "specificity" of the test. Sensitivity measures the proportion of actual positives that are correctly identified as such, or true positive. Specificity measures the proportion of original negatives that are correctly identified as true negative. So, if the test is 70 percent specific, this means it could be falsely negative in 30 percent of the time when it should be positive. To check whether the test is truly positive or negative, the provider may send the sample for confirmation, which is generally done by liquid chromatography–mass spectrometry (LCMS).

Another important factor is the metabolism of the drug in the specific individual. An individual may metabolize a particular drug faster due to genetic differences or other medications he or she is taking simultaneously. A fast metabolizer metabolizes particular medicine quicker than those who are slow metabolizers. On the other hand, some medicines inhibit enzymes that are required for metabolism. Metabolism is unique to each individual, determined by genetic and environmental factors. Genetic polymorphisms of the CYP450 2D6 enzyme can cause individuals to be poor or rapid metabolizers of opioids and other drugs metabolized by those enzymes.

Environmental influences further complicate metabolism. For example, coadministered drugs that are also metabolized by CYP450 enzymes used by the opioids or that inhibit CYP450 2D6, causing decreased metabolism. When the prosecutor introduced this subject in the closing argument, we rebutted and showed urine toxicology results on placards. The counterargument that the state prosecutor projected as negative was actually positive when you follow the characteristics of metabolism. Even absent results would not indicate one direction, though diversion is one of the possibilities. They neglected to discuss results with the defense during the hearing examination and instead drew inaccurate conclusions on their own.

We indicated our stance and argument in the "Exceptions," noting that it required expert testimony to determine whether a patient should have been dealt with more harshly or whether particular toxicology should have led a reasonable provider to conclude that action had to be taken because of evidence of drug diversion. Again, the reason was that even experts who read and analyze urine toxicology results acknowledge that interpreting these tests are challenging and usually do not suggest a definitive course of action.

Regarding the diversion, the practice used all the precautionary means available at the time. For example, all the prescriptions required a raised-seal stamp signed by the provider, the name of the pharmacy allowed to fill said prescription, copies of a prescription in the chart, and tamper-proof prescription pads. We also used random urine toxicologies, and in suspected cases, urine samples were taken under direct observation. There was an audit to institute pill counting if any concern of diversion was raised. It was routine procedure to discharge patients if they failed consistent compliance. Additionally, pharmacy profiles were reviewed. Interestingly, the prosecutor did not present any evidence where the failure of the system resulted in the diversion.

When Dr. Ward was asked during cross-examination how many times he was faced with this very scenario—where a pregnant patient came to his office for pain management (i.e., a patient who came into his practice on methadone and got pregnant), he admitted that he was only faced with this "two, three times." Also of significance, when Dr. Ward was asked if he could cite one article that would support the opinion that he had just given, he said, "I don't review OB literature on a regular basis. If you—you know, I could look for one, but no. Right off the top of my head, I can't cite one."

In contrast, Dr. Kabazie, an expert called by the defense, wholeheartedly agreed it is within the standard of care to continue pregnant patients on their pain medication. Pregnancy is not a punishment. A doctor should not take the patient off pain medications on which she has relied. What would happen if a pregnant patient was forced to stop pain medications, even slowly, now that she had to bear pregnancy and suffer pain without any pain medications? In that situation, Dr. Kabazie's testimony was unequivocal. It would be medical negligence to wean the mother off opioid pain medication, and it may even be appropriate to increase pain medications, if necessary, depending on the level of pain, as the pregnancy got closer to the end of the third trimester. According to the hearing officer, there should be a document in the records, the pluses and minuses of continuing medications at present levels needed to control the mother's pain after she got pregnant. Such a document is the Pain Contractor Agreement, clearly written and signed by the patients that continuing pain medications could be harmful to newborn babies, who are required to go through the withdrawal process. Unfortunately, once a patient who is on opioids becomes pregnant, there may be limited options of getting her off the pain medication.

The final breach in the standard of care to which Dr. Ward testified had to do with documentation. A general opinion was that, based on *his* review of the patient files, there was "a gross disconnect" or what he called "the total absence of documentation" to support the standard of care. Again, he gave this opinion despite having a practice completely different from my practice. First, he estimated that the average duration he treated a patient was six months. Second, by his own admission, Dr. Ward received the twenty-seven voluminous files one week or less before the hearing. In fact, he admitted that if the files had arrived before that, he had not looked at them.

As written in the "Exceptions," the chief hearing officer's reliance on the model policy, which admittedly was not "religiously" followed, was given too much weight in his recommendation. As the chief hearing officer himself acknowledged in the recommendation, the model policy was not adopted as an actual regulation in Delaware until February 2012. Prior to February 2012, the model policy was to have served only as a "guideline" for pain specialists like me.

In fact, during the relevant time frame in this case, Dr. Kabazie referred to a book written by Scott Fishman, MD, titled *Responsible Opioid Prescribing: A Physician Guide*, which was entered into evidence. Dr. Kabazie agreed with Dr. Fishman's observation noted in the book:

That although the Model Policy represents the most concise consensus guidelines for safe opioid prescribing, until now this document has not been translated into practical terms for clinical Practice. Consequently, few physicians are familiar with these guidelines, and even fewer utilize them in their practice.

At the hearing, Dr. Kabazie fully endorsed the comment made on page 103 of the book that "[t]he FSMB (Federation of State Medical Board's Model Policy for the Use of Controlled Substances for the Treatment of Pain) does not set a standard of medical practice."

Dr. Kabazie testified that a guideline like the model policy, however, does not take away a physician's judgment as it relates to the treatment of patient, which means that a guideline does not have to be followed in order to meet standard of care, as opposed to being considered when treating a patient.

The chief hearing officer next took issue with the fact that I had failed to prepare in the records an acceptable treatment plan for my patients, consistent with the model policy.

Another concern he raised and noted in the recommendation was, "One of the reasons for detailed records is to maximize the chances that subsequent providers who pick up a chart would have the information necessary to make treatment decisions." However, no expert opinions were presented at the hearing that the lack of documentation, by either respondent contained in the Tri-State's medical records, ever caused harm to any of the twenty-seven patients whose medical records were entered into evidence.

This finding by the hearing officer was rebutted and written in the "Exceptions." The specific finding by the chief hearing officer was: "Dr. Niaz testified that Tri-State typically forwarded new providers records of the previous 3-4 visits to the receiving physicians." There was no testimony presented by the state, who had the burden of proof, that any subsequent health care provider's ability to treat a former patient of Tri-State was compromised. No health care provider of any patients of Tri-State was ever dissatisfied with the medical information received, and the medical information received on a patient in no way hindered the ability of that subsequent health care provider to treat that patient. If true, such proof would appear to be easily obtainable through testimony from one or more of the subsequent health care providers (or even a patient), if they felt they were not provided with adequate information or received ambiguous or misleading information to treat a patient. At the very least, this should have been a subject of expert testimony that it occurred to one or more specific patients, as opposed to leaving it to pure speculation that "glitches" in certain EMR records could potentially mislead a subsequent health care provider.

The next major criticism cited by the chief hearing officer had to do with the need to offer patients referrals or other treatment modalities or rehabilitation programs. It was a general statement and should have been patient-specific. Every patient did not need a referral, as all had gone through this process and were on a maintenance treatment. Many patients' consultation records were presented. As with all the other allegations not specifically mentioned during the hearing, this topic should have been brought out during the hearing and discussed with the defense. Instead, it came out after the hearing was concluded. The chief hearing officer explicitly recognized that I treated a patient population of limited financial means. These economic limitations made it difficult for this population to pay for other care modalities, such as physical therapy, orthopedic or psychiatric consultations, certain medications, and other forms of care. In fact, he recognized that "there was some testimony that few if any, orthopedists and psychiatrists in the geographic area served by Tri-State were willing to examine or treat Tri-State patients because of their modest resources or Medicaid status."

The chief hearing officer's next criticism had to do with the alleged failure to document the "presence of one or more recognized medical indications for the use of a controlled substance." The state offered no concise opinion or authoritative statement as to what would be a recognized medical indication. During the hearing, the prosecutor asked the nurse practitioner why she prescribed pain medications to a patient whose diagnosis was herpes zoster, which can be a very painful condition, but according to the prosecutor, this was not a recognized medical condition for which to write pain medications. What was the basis of her arguments? Nobody knows. The nurse practitioner informed her that herpetic neuralgia could be very painful. In fact, this painful condition can clearly be proven. Even a quick search on the internet would demonstrate the pain ramifications.

The chief hearing officer concluded that I must have thought these patients were being medicated too aggressively and that had I more closely reviewed their charts during their treatment with Tri-State, a different conclusion could have been made.

He was responding to the action taken by the nurse practitioner to restrict her prescription writing on pain medications. He was looking at one of the spectra of treatments but not realizing that many of the patients were inherited from other doctors on a high dosage of pain medications. It was not at our discretion to suddenly stop or curtail pain medications. These patients relied on medicines to perform their daily activities.

The chief hearing officer next took issue with the following: "Dr. Niaz failed to prepare in the records an acceptable treatment plan for his patients consistent with the Model Policy." In our old EMR, this was under the heading of "Recommendations"; it was never a law that the title must be "Treatment Plan."

The chief hearing officer specifically found: "Dr. Niaz did not discuss the risks and benefits of the use of controlled substances with patients." He made this specific finding even though he acknowledged that the patient files contained a pain management agreement that touched on this subject. The pain management agreement included informed consent regarding the side effects of these medications. Obviously, the benefits of medicines were also evident, as patients' functional capacity improved, and often they started to work again and performed gainful activities. Since these side effects were written on the pain management agreement, I did not feel obligated to write in detail and mention each side effect, particularly the side effects documented in the PDR, which is extremely comprehensive and inclusive of even minor details found in animals. It is not possible to discuss every piece of information written in PDR with the patient. Only essential and common side effects are discussed.

The utilization of a pain management contract was also ignored. The chief hearing officer acknowledged that most patients signed the pain management contracts but concluded that "they were just another document in the chart." He noted that breaches in pain contracts were found, and he cited that these were either ignored or not pursued with reasonable diligence. Once again, the state presented no expert testimony regarding the reasonableness of giving patients second and third chances to do what the providers believed, in their clinical judgment, was the correct course of action when there were breaches in the pain management contract.

Pain agreements done for pain management are somewhat different in their applications, compared to the language of a generic legal document. Here, the provider or a physician makes a decision in the interest of the patient. If, for example, urine toxicology is not consistent and has to be dealt with in clinical circumstances, a layman may think the provider has ignored a visible sign of drug abuse. This type of issue should have been specifically brought forward in the hearing for discussion to get my input and to hear my side of the story and the implications to patient care. For fair adjudication, there needed to be testimony by the experts and by me before concluding them as facts and issues of negligence, forwarded to the Deliberation Committee.

The chief hearing officer appeared to be surprised by this finding when the evidence was presented. He had specifically noted that when he reviewed the amended complaint, he had assumed that claims of 'overprescription would be prominent. However, despite this assumption, the chief hearing officer specifically noted, "that proved not to be the case."

Our "Exceptions to the Facts and Findings" was hand-delivered to the licensing board. We covered almost every finding declared by the hearing officer as a violation of the standard of care. We were confident that since the Deliberation Committee had medically trained professionals, they would understand things that were difficult to analyze with application in real medical practice by the hearing officer. There was, however, the necessity of time. As Deliberation Committee members were volunteers, there might be time constraints that would prevent a thorough review of our "Exceptions." All Deliberation Committee members were to be neutral, and I continued to pray for justice and respect for all regulations.

CHAPTER 11

A few months passed as we anxiously waited for the Deliberation Committee to give their verdict. As defense, we had filed our detailed and persuasive "Exceptions." The prosecutor also submitted their exceptions to the findings of the hearing officer. The hearing officer recommended putting my medical license under probation for three years, but the prosecutor wanted to put it under suspension or revoke the license. Our "Exceptions" suggested that should have been based on references, but instead, the prosecutor reiterated the allegations. There seemed to be an interest in dwelling on the current recommendations by the hearing officer and an interest to sever the action by the Deliberation Committee.

Waiting for the result was not easy. Members of the Deliberation Committee were expected to carefully examine all pieces of evidence presented by the hearing officer and the exceptions to the findings of the hearing officer. We were, appropriately, waiting for justice. Many of the members of the committee were physicians. They should have been neutral, with have no prior participation in investigations or any links to any investigator or the prosecutor. The committee met monthly and posted the meeting's minutes online after each session. We checked the minutes each month as we waited to see when my case would be reviewed. Their task was to examine the entire portfolio of documents and pieces of evidence presented in the case, and, after thorough discussion, come up with conclusions, based on governing laws at the time. Their decision could be appealed in the Superior Court within a month after deliberation.

The primary objectives of the Delaware Board of Medical Licensure and Discipline are to promote public health, safety, and welfare and to protect the public from the unprofessional, improper, unauthorized, or unqualified practice of medicine and certain other health care professions. We remained confident that the decision by the Deliberation Committee would fall in our favor.

After a couple of months, the decision by the Deliberation Committee was announced. Again, it was a headline in the major newspapers. The licensing board wanted to make an example of this verdict to warn other pain-management doctors and therefore invited the media and briefed them on the outcome. The Deliberation Committee followed the recommendation of the prosecutor and suspended my medical license for three years. The Public Order is outlined below:

> Pursuant to 29 Del. C a properly noticed hearing was conducted before a hearing office ... The Board is bound by the findings of fact made by the hearing officer. However, the Board may affirm or modify the hearing officer's conclusions of law and recommended a penalty. ... Dr. Niaz also forwarded exceptions to the hearing officer's recommendation, ... Dr. Niaz criticizes many of the findings of fact made by the hearing officer as inconsistent with the testimony at the hearing or not supported by the totality of the evidence. Pursuant to 29 Del. C., this Board is bound by the findings of fact made by the hearing officer and cannot alter these findings. ... [The] disciplinary Hearing filed by the State against him was a public hearing and the public documents produced therefrom "bring discredit upon the medical profession" are in direct conflict with the expert testimony provided and do not express an adequate foundation at law (e.g., finding that the burden of persuasion shifted to Dr. Niaz to provide therapeutic bases for his prescriptive order, and that Dr. Niaz provided testimony regarding such bases, but that such testimony was insufficient to carry this burden, without citation to any legal authority,

improperly imposed respondent superior liability on Dr. Niaz for the action of Ms. Binkley, an Advance Practice Nurse. … The Board deliberated on the hearing officer's recommendation on February 13, 2013. In this case, the hearing officer found that Dr. Niaz failed to properly train and supervise his staff. … Specifically, the Board finds that Dr. Niaz's deviation from the standard in his record-keeping and charting. … If the APN is an employee, the doctor is the "captain of the ship," and therefore, Dr. Niaz is held responsible for the practices of Ms. Binkley while she was working in his office. … Dr. Niaz criticizes many of the findings of fact made by the hearing officer as inconsistent with the testimony at the Hearing or not supported by the totality of the evidence. Pursuant to 29 Del C. § 8735, this Board is bound by the findings of fact made by the hearing officer and cannot alter these findings. Dr. Niaz argues that the chief hearing officer's conclusions of law use circular reasoning. … improperly imposed respondent superior liability on Dr. Niaz for the action of Ms. Binkley, an Advance Practice Nurse with her own independent prescriptive authority; overly relied on the Model Policy for the Use of Controlled Substances for the Treatment of Pain when such policy was not adopted by this Board until February 2012. … did not properly take into account that the State provided no evidence of any patient harm incurred. … The Board finds this is different than a truly independently practicing APN, and therefore, Dr. Niaz should be held responsible for Ms. Binkley's prescribing practices.

This was shocking to us. The decision of the Deliberation Committee was beyond our imagination. First, why was the board "bound by the findings of fact made by the hearing officer"? Again, the hearing officer was a nonmedical person, and his opinion could be wrong. His responsibility was to gather all evidence provided by the defense and prosecution, interpret the law based on such information, and then forward it to the

Deliberation Committee. He was expected to apply the conclusion of the law based on the evidence presented at the hearing. Unfortunately, he acted as an expert in medicine and started interpreting charts with his limited understanding.

Second, the Deliberation Committee stated that the "burden of persuasion was shifted to Dr. Niaz." This was a new piece of news and an unfortunate loophole in the law. The case was simple. The prosecutor had to prove by evidence, and she failed to do so. Still, the hearing officer ignored their impartiality as they overtly showed deference to the state and the prosecutor so they could win the case. The way they did this was to shift the burden of proof to the defense. What? Huh? How was this legal? Shouldn't there be some rules and regulations governing these decisions? How could they just shift the burden of proof like that? Was there is a precedent?

The hearing officer also had to state what *the defense should prove.* At the beginning of the case, he announced that the prosecutor had the burden of proof. After the hearing, shifting the burden of proof proved the case by twisting facts. We were never provided the information that the burden of proof had shifted to us. At deliberation, the burden was shifted. It was as if the court ordered the defense to remain quiet, and then, at the deliberation, the judge announced that since the defense did not say anything, that meant the prosecution had won the case.

The expert brought by the state was completely biased, and he agreed that he only browsed through the charts. On the other hand, the expert brought by the defense was a professor and a program director of a pain medicine program at a teaching university. I can only conclude that the testimony from a defense expert was utterly ignored by the board.

Further, the board made me liable for not training or supervising the nurse practitioner, who had independent prescriptive authority. Why had the board issued her independent prescriptive authority if she was not qualified? A collaborative physician is required to have a contract ensuring that he or she will be available to the nurse practitioner in need of consultation. A physician is not expected to provide any training to the nurse practitioner. According to Title 24, Laws of the State of Delaware, training is required for those staff like med-tech or a front desk person, not a professional nurse practitioner who has completed training and was awarded a medical license, as well as a DEA license, to practice independently.

The model policy regarding documentation proposed by the Federation of State Medical Boards was merely a suggestion prior to 2009. It was a severe error for the Deliberation Committee to rest the conclusion on the model policy. It showed they did not bother to thoroughly read the hearing officer's finding, who never stated such a thing in his conclusion.

The defense focused only on allegations in the hearing that were raised by the prosecutor. In fact, any allegation raised was effectively defended, and counter pieces of evidence were provided. My testimony was concise and lasted approximately an hour because the prosecutor did not bother to question any allegation with me. The prosecutor submitted the selected portion of the medical records to the hearing officer and let him decide on his own about any deficiency. The defense attorney then went through charts linked to my care. To justify disciplinary action, the Deliberation Committee had to shift the burden of proof to the defense after the hearing, which was an excellent example of malicious prosecution.

Regarding the defense's "Exceptions to the Facts and Findings," the Deliberation Committee stated they were "inconsistent with the testimony at the Hearing or not supported by the totality of the evidence." A total negation of facts was provided by the defense in "Exceptions," as well as expert testimony by the defense. They labeled me the "Captain of the Ship," so, therefore, I should be penalized for what they inaccurately considered a lack of supervision of the nurse practitioner.

The board's decision was a public document. The prosecution, to advance their program agenda, wanted to publish the decision in the news. It was, therefore, the heading in the local newspapers. The next day, this was the talk of the town. People were calling, and even newspaper reporters asked me to give my input. I kept silent. It is my firm faith that if someone does an injustice, the almighty God will ultimately bring forward the truth.

Our next step was to approach the Medical Society of Delaware to find a strategy to get justice. They agreed to review the case and the findings of the hearing officer, which we forwarded. They responded in a letter, written by Dr. Kushner, the president of the Medical Society:

> On behalf of the Medical Society of Delaware, I am writing to you as Counsel to Muhammed A. Niaz, MD, concerning actions taken by the Delaware Board of Medical Licensing and Discipline against Dr. Niaz's medical License at its meeting on February 5, 2013.
>
> After familiarizing ourselves with the facts and circumstances of Dr. Niaz's case, weighing the pressing need for responsible and stable pain management practices in Delaware, and discussing the matter with the Society's lawyer, Mr. Battaglia, we strongly urge you as Counsel to Dr. Niaz, to respectfully request the Board's reconsideration of its orders concerning the Dr. Niaz matter.
>
> While together, we all must work tirelessly and aggressively in shutting down pill mills, we must work equally as diligently in supporting responsible pain management and cultivating trusted practices which are necessary to curbing diversion and abuse. Thus, in the view of the Society, the actions taken by the BMLD addressing aspects of the matter considering your client appear to be unwarranted and unjust.

Once a medical license is restricted in one state, other states where a physician or a nurse practitioner has an active medical license will take reciprocal action. I started getting certified mail announcing intention of reciprocal action. The newspapers in other states also broadcast the news, displaying it in very spicy and inflating language to get attention and showing it in headlines, such as in the *Cecil Whig* and *Newark Post* newspapers. That generated a panicked reaction in the community at large. Patients started calling the office about their medical records and their ongoing care, asking who would take them from there onward and whether the subsequent doctor would provide the same respect. I could not answer any such questions, as there was no backup set up. I worked to arrange for another physician to take over my patients so they would have continuity of care. It was daring for me to go to the office, as many patients who did not have appointments were waiting to probe the details.

The other major issue was to find a pharmacy that would continue to fill prescriptions; it was an uphill task. Most pharmacies did not want to take the risk of litigation, so it was easy to deny filling prescriptions. Many patients were elderly, and they could not go far to find another doctor, as most doctors refused to prescribe any pain medication. In the town where I was practicing in Maryland, no doctor dared to prescribe pain medication except in very acute conditions and for a concise time. People cursed the regulating authorities for leaving them stranded. My practice was minimal, and a couple of pharmacists who knew me personally continued to work with me—but still in high-alert mode. One of the pharmacists, Ms. Mary Beth, owner of Lyon's Pharmacy, Elkton, Maryland, came to my office to further discuss providing care. On questioning, she informed me that the investigators from regulating authorities had threatened her from time to time regarding filling these prescriptions.

I inquired what they were threatening, as these prescriptions were not illegal. She answered that in their eyes, all the prescriptions were wrong and overprescribed.

I asked, "Do they have any medical knowledge?"

"No," she replied. They were essentially nonmedical people who were enraged by their organizations, like the DEA, so they were adamant that all these prescriptions were wrong.

Soon, the regulating authorities would take adverse action. I spent more than an hour discussing patient care and tried to persuade her to continue filling the prescriptions and even went through some of the charts she mentioned and showed that I reduced medications. These patients had taken very high dosages in the past when prescribing pain medications was unrestricted. The goal was a slow reduction, to which these patients could agree and tolerate. The standard of care is to reduce the medication gradually, as they can handle it. Reducing their pain medications was threatening. Often, they became furious because this was the only thing that was keeping them alive and functional in their eyes. They had been on these medications for decades, like taking blood pressure and diabetes medication.

Ms. Mary Beth informed me that the investigators were collecting all the pharmacy profiles and any other documents linked to my prescriptions. It was time-consuming for a pharmacist. Why would a pharmacist go to such trouble? The easy solution was to deny filling the prescription.

After discussion with Ms. Mary Beth, I did not know whether this was a notice given indirectly to stop writing pain medications or just cautious advice. I wished I could stop writing all these pain medications, but I knew it would be fatal, as a few people already had died after I stopped prescribing pain medications from the Delaware office. If I did the same in Elkton, the result would be the same.

I was in the office working when one of the staff, Mrs. Sarah Forbes, asked me, "Who is this Dr. Stephen Cooper?"

"He's an ENT doctor. Why do you ask?"

"He was the one who convinced the Deliberation Committee to suspend your medical license."

The chief investigator, Mr. Brady, had said in the emergency hearing that Dr. Cooper was a co-investigator. Mrs. Forbes had reviewed the minutes of the licensing board and shared the minutes with me. They should note the co-investigator was a sitting member of the Deliberation Committee. I could not believe the licensing board allowed an investigator to sit in on the deliberation. It was clearly written in the committee's laws that no one who was part of the investigation was allowed to sit on the committee that deliberated on that same case.

The minutes also indicated that the discussion lasted just a few minutes. How could they discuss all the findings, which involved thousands of pages, including the "Facts and Findings" by the hearing officer, the "Exceptions to the Facts and Findings," and other related documents in such a short period? It was quite obvious that the decision was predetermined. It was the ultimate conclusion to the witch hunt, providing a sacrificial lamb for the state's agenda. The deliberation was a mere formality and not a legitimate exercise for fair and equitable findings. They wanted to punish a pain doctor and declare a warning to all doctors who prescribed pain medications.

Another fishy thing mentioned in the minutes was that the deliberation occurred behind closed doors. Why? The entire proceedings, from the beginning, had been public. It started with a news headline; the hearing was public, but no one was allowed to sit in on the deliberation. They needed a deliberation meeting behind closed doors to manipulate decisions. It was utterly offensive that they were able to discuss the case and conclude that my license should be suspended within a few minutes. This was a severe violation of due process and justice. Again, an investigator should not sit in on the deliberation.

I called my attorney and informed him of our findings so he could begin working on filing a complaint. He sent an email to the board, and, as required, a copy of that email was sent to the prosecutor. The prosecutor subsequently disclosed another name, Dr. Col-Morgan, a gynecologist who also participated in the investigation and also participated in the deliberation. Again, this was a total violation of due process. What kind of deliberating body was this? How fair and just could they be if they could not even follow their governing regulations? The state's underlying strategy to win the case was now bubbling to the surface. How many others who participated as investigators were not cleared and made known? After all, the Deliberation Committee was a group of people who might meet and discuss outside the licensing board's premises. This was clearly revealed by the time they spent in the discussion of my case, as noted in the meeting's minutes—"a few minutes."

It became clear that the entire Deliberation Committee, with perhaps an exception of a few, were either tainted by discussion with others or had directly participated in the initial investigation. Why was an ENT doctor, who never practiced pain management or internal medicine, a co-investigator in this case? A gynecologist who participated in the investigation and then sat in on the deliberation would not be without reason. Their reasoning was unjust. They planned to win the case by hook or by crook. This formed multiple barriers for the defense to cross. If the prosecutor and the hearing officer failed to convince the Deliberation Committee to suspend my medical license, then the investigators sitting on the Deliberation Committee would do that. With this extra level of prosecutorial leverage, the state would not lose the case.

One might ask what interest they had in doing all these things. The answer is straightforward. As I've mentioned, they wanted to make this a case that would serve as a notice to all other doctors who prescribed pain medications. There also was a personal interest in gaining a better position to influence political benefits. They likely thought if doctors stopped prescribing pain medications, then the problem of the drug epidemic could be resolved—or, at the very least, suppressed. Furthermore, it would be a star on their résumé to say they were making diligent efforts to combat the opioid crisis.

I wondered why they never discussed any case with me, before or during the hearing. The answer was simple. They needed a scapegoat. It was apparent that they were cooperating together and building a cascade of cooperation to win the case.

Now, we had two options: request that the licensing board redeliberate the case, or knock on the door of the Superior Court for justice. The appeal had to be completed within a month. We immediately filed an appeal in the Superior Court. After reviewing the case and communicating with the prosecutor, who had no objection to issuing a no-motion order, the Superior Court issued the no-motion order. This order served as an endorsement by the prosecutor that due process was violated.

The licensing board was also informed about investigators sitting in on the deliberation. They agreed to redeliberate the case but wanted to redeliberate with the same committee, minus two members who would be excused to sit out of the deliberation room but would be present in the vicinity. We objected to having the same Deliberation Committee redeliberate, as they, at the very least, were tainted by bias from the prior inappropriate committee. How many members sitting in on the deliberation actually participated in the investigation but were never disclosed? What were their findings? Two names were accidentally revealed, but the actual number was never published. In our minds, redeliberation would be to endorse that their earlier decision was correct. How could we trust them to make a fair and impartial recommendation after their gross and obvious errors? It seemed unlikely that the same members who apparently agreed on suspension would now agree that they were wrong. It was like proving yourself wrong. We conveyed our opinion and expected that a different Deliberation Committee would be selected. The licensing board refused our request.

The attorney general himself realized what was going on under his nose. He may have been struggling with his own health, as he was suddenly diagnosed with brain cancer. He realized injustice was going on in his office, so he decided to terminate the services of the prosecutor. This initiated an active communication between my attorney and the new prosecutor. I wished they had developed this communication before setting up a hearing; it would have resolved all their concerns.

Last but not least, the termination of the prosecutor was the glimmer of hope that justice was possible. My attorney informed me of the change, and this sounded like my victory. I was glad, as the new prosecutor was humble and willing to participate in a mutual way to terminate this case as soon as possible. I was also financially broke and almost had lost any hope of getting back to practice. As Martin Luther King Jr. said, "We must accept finite disappointment but never lose infinite hope."

CHAPTER 12

After reviewing the case, the new prosecutor offered to take a case off entirely. That gave us a glimmer of hope and sounded like the end of the story. Unfortunately, it also implied a risk that they would redo the investigation and the entire litigation again. That might take many more years. My limitation was a financial burden, as I was paying the current lawsuit on credit. I did not know how I would even pay those loans; even if I sold my office building, I would still be broke. Bankruptcy was another option to consider.

Further delay would limit my credit options. Almost all insurance companies had already discontinued coverage requests or issued notices of potential cancellation of coverage. Financially, I had to make decisions in consideration of the security of my economic and personal future. I could not afford any delay. If they redid the entire process, it would take years to end the litigation. During this period, I would not be able to work, as insurance providers had already left, and they would not provide privileges or any contract. Even malpractice insurance would not continue. The only answer was to end this litigation.

We informed them of our concern and indicated that we wanted to finish the case. After a thorough discussion between the prosecutor and the defense attorney, we mutually agreed to sign a consent agreement to resolve the case. In the consent agreement, both parties agreed on no disciplinary action and agreed that the licensing board could ask to review my patients' medical charts at any time. Further, they decided that the documentation was deficient due to the problem in the electronic medical record. The consent agreement noted that those deficiencies had been fixed. The agreement explained,

> The documentation problems caused by the EMR system utilized during the relevant period at Dr. Niaz office (Tri-State) was the result of a computer program purchased in good faith years ago only to have the manufacturer of the computer system file for bankruptcy resulting in no technical support being available to the office.

They further noted that a new system had been purchased, and the problem had been solved.

In the agreement, it was also agreed:

> At any time after the restoration of his CSR, Dr. Niaz grants access to the Board or its designee to randomly selected charts of patients for whom medical care has been provided by Dr. Niaz during the immediately preceding 90 days and from which last names of the applicable patients have been deleted, to determine whether the deficiencies admitted herein have been remedied.

Both parties agreed to sign the consent agreement. The licensing board could access the charts of any physician, so our agreeing to that would not make any significant difference. They wanted to have something written in their favor; it was a compromise, but at least we could go back to work. We were confident that the case would end now.

To make it legal, it had to be approved by the Deliberation Committee of the licensing board, who had made the earlier decision. The consent agreement was officially submitted to the licensing board to have a motion. The board decided to discuss the consent agreement in their regularly scheduled meeting.

We understood the critical nature of this consent agreement, particularly when the same board had decided on a suspension order just a couple of months ago. They might consider it a decision that proved them wrong, resulting in an affront to them individually and, perhaps, some bruised egos. We requested the board to allow us to speak a few minutes to the Deliberation Committee. This was very important, as we knew the committee had a totally different perspective of the case in their minds. We wanted to balance this perspective. We wanted to show the true picture.

We attended the meeting but our request to speak to the committee was denied. The consent agreement was rejected by the Deliberation Committee, and they opted to redeliberate the case. This response was unexpected. Why was it rejected, when the prosecutor had agreed to the consent agreement? Action speaks louder than words; they wanted another opportunity to defend their earlier decision and advance their program agenda. If they had fully accepted consent agreement, it would have also confirmed their biased deliberation the first time; in the first deliberation, they reportedly discussed revocation or suspension of my medical license, and now the consent agreement was for no disciplinary action.

Redeliberation took place in a few days; this time, at least, they had discussion among themselves. During deliberation, two investigators were requested to sit outside. In the second deliberation, they concluded they would put my medical license on probation for three years, in addition to agreeing to the other recommendations of the hearing officer.

I was not happy with the probation decision because I tried to help stranded patients and patients left by other doctors. I expected that they would appreciate my kindness. If there were deficiencies in documentation or otherwise, it could be discussed, and that would provide me with an education that could improve our performance—no error was done intentionally. If I counted the amount of money lost in litigation, it would be in the millions, as it was not just the amount paid for one litigation process. One litigation led to another litigation, like a ripple effect, so I faced multiple litigations. Also, counting the amount of time lost by not practicing or practicing at a minimum added to the cost.

Losing dignity is immeasurable. This was only one state, and I had licenses in three states, which would add to litigation costs, as reciprocal action would be forthcoming that required legal fees to defend. As for my Pennsylvania license, I would not have the money to hire an attorney, so I decided to defend the case myself.

Interestingly, when they called for a hearing, they printed out all the allegations they had found through the Delaware Licensing Board, so I had to prepare to duplicate the hearing process. The litigation process also occurred against many insurance providers, as many insurance providers denied coverage. Some insurance providers also assumed that the medical service was never provided and asked for reimbursement.

I faced a hearing in front of a panel selected by a well-known insurance provider. They did not limit their questions to the allegations but asked questions related to my medical knowledge, as if I was not mentally fit to practice medicine.

Every day, a new front could open. I kept all the documents and summaries handy as I was sending information to different agencies and insurance companies almost every day. The Board of Internal Medicine wanted to suspend my board certification and asked me to inform them why they should not do so. I had to write a defense document, approximately twenty pages long, with multiple reference letters and documents to convince them not to curtail my board certification. The most challenging thing was that every organization gave limited time to respond or appeal, and the amount of documentation required to convince them was enormous, so I had to stay late into the night and continue working in the daytime to meet deadlines. I am thankful to some of my staff, like Mrs. Nicole Karavan, Mrs. Kimberly, and Mrs. Sarah Forbes, for helping me gather related information and helping me with documentation.

Continuing malpractice insurance was also a nightmare. Finally, there was a disciplinary action, and that could be enough reason to deny malpractice coverage. I had to face another hearing with the malpractice insurance provider. During the hearing, I convinced them that the practice enforced all safe means to prevent any malpractice suits. I thought, *You guys never paid a single penny during the litigation. You were acting mercifully to continue my malpractice insurance.* I realized that beggars can't be choosers. I had paid them thousands of dollars since I started practicing medicine. Still, it was at their discretion to choose to provide malpractice insurance.

Every day was a battle with ups and downs. I struggled to cross one hurdle after another. Some days, it looked like I would have to shut down my medical practice, while on other days, I might receive a glimpse of hope. I was floating on a sea, with wave after wave tossing me in a direction that I was unsure of. I was being dragged to an unknown destination.

We had the option to go back to the Superior Court and get another no-motion order and reverse the decision. This seemed reasonable, as the prosecutor had already agreed to the consent agreement. A drawback, however, was that even if the Superior Court decided in favor of our appeal, the Superior Court would have to refer the case back to the licensing board to redo the deliberation or even the entire process. The Superior Court could not do deliberation for the licensing board; It has to be done by a licensing board. The board was adamant about keeping the same Deliberation Committee that had already deliberated twice. Expecting they would reach a different result the third time was unrealistic. The only good thing about the deliberation was that it ended the case. We could plan for the future.

If the case started with the intent of fairness and justice, then my thought was it would be a headline in the leading newspapers, reporting the new turn of events in my favor. But there was no news. Such was a violation of due process, but the story never even reached the media. How much is media-controlled and biased? It was never mentioned in any report that due process or the deliberation process was violated with the two investigators sitting in the deliberation. This violation should have warranted reporting in the newspaper, yet it was not mentioned, not even a small article in the paper.

After the conclusion of my case, the nurse practitioner's case was scheduled to be deliberated by the Joint Commission of the Nursing Board. The trial occurred, and I was placed again in my role as captain of the ship by the Deliberation Committee. Again, her performance was linked to my deficiency in training her and my not providing subsequent supervision. Deliberation by the Joint Commission was very interesting, as their conclusions contradicted most of the significant findings of the hearing officer, as well as the Deliberation Committee. They wrote in a document:

Before the Delaware Joint Practice Committee

The Joint Practice Committee is bound by the findings of fact made by the hearing officer ... The hearing officer's next conclusion is that Ms. Binkley violated 19 Del. C, 1922 in that she is "unfit or incompetent by reason of negligence, habits or other causes" to practice advance practice nursing. In so finding, the hearing officer concluded, as a matter of law, that Ms. Binkley's practices while employed by Dr. Niaz clearly demonstrated unfitness and incompetency by reason of her professional negligence. The Committee rejects this conclusion of Law. **The hearing officer's conclusion of law, that Ms. Binkley's practices constituted professional negligence is in error. The hearing officer noted many of his own perceived "flaws"** with Ms. Binkley's charting practices, and the Committee agrees the charts were not perfect. However, the charts included in Ms. Binkley's Exceptions to the hearing officer's recommendation do not rise to the level of professional negligence. Ms. Binkley's charts do contain histories. There may not be a physical exam noted at every pain management meeting, but this is not required, and the hearing officer's reliance on this omission in finding professional negligence is contrary to the standard of care. ...

The Committee accepts the hearing officer's finding that the practice demonstrated a lot of effort into getting urine toxicology screens and that more could have been done with the information. However, the Committee rejects the hearing officer's conclusion of law that Ms. Binkley failed to provide the degree of care that a reasonably prudent and careful Registered Nurse and Advanced Practice Nurse would employ in similar circumstances. ...

Contrary to the hearing officer's conclusion that Ms. Binkley negligently practiced was due to failure to coordinate with other treating providers, the exceptions filed by Ms. Binkley included many exhibits introduced at the Hearing that demonstrate Ms. Binkley was interacting with primary care physicians of some of her patients.

The Committee accepts the hearing officer's finding that the practice demonstrated a lot of effort into getting urine toxicology screens and that more could have been done with the information. However, the Committee rejects the hearing officer's conclusion of law that Ms. Binkley failed to provide the degree of care that a reasonably prudent and careful Registered Nurse and Advanced Practice Nurse would employ in similar circumstances. "The records demonstrate that toxicology screen results were used as a starting off point for a conversation with a patient and that Dr. Niaz's stated policy regarding discharging patients who violate their pain management contracts was also reasonable." …

With regard to the hearing officer's finding that Ms. Binkley's treatment of ADD demonstrated professional negligence due to her "failure" to order appropriate "psychological or psychiatric testing or referrals out," (Hearing officer recommendation at 210), the Committee rejects this finding as there is hardly any testing available for adult ADD, and the hearing officer recommendation does not indicate any evidence of any such available testing was provided. "**Ms. Binkley's practice, as outlined by the hearing officer's factual findings, were within the acceptable standard of care.**"

The Committee rejects the hearing officer's finding that Ms. Binkley engaged in professional negligence by failing to order other treatment modalities, and failing to chart appropriate "Treatment Plans" the exceptions submitted by Ms. Binkley include some of the exhibits provided to the hearing officer, and these exhibits clearly indicate outside treatment modalities were ordered. The availability of other treatment modalities are also limited by Medicaid and what it will pay for. The Committee is aware, although the hearing officer may not have been, that a lot of testing cannot be completed because those tests are expensive and will not be covered. … **Also, doctors' orders can be seen on every case chart, and doctors' orders are considered a treatment plan for the APN. It is not known what else the hearing officer was looking for.** In short, the hearing officer's expectation for "treatment plan" is not generally acceptable practice. The patients are being seen every month, which is a high standard. Follow up plans are present in these charts, and the Committee suspects **the hearing officer doesn't know how medical charts work in actual practice.** The charts are not confusing as the hearing officer made them out to be in his order to the licensed professionals on the Committee. Risks and benefits are explained in the pain contract, as seen in the exceptions provided to the Committee and presented as evidence to the hearing officer. It also cannot go without being noted that there was no factual finding that Ms. Binkley prescribed controlled substances to patients in amounts that exceed safe therapeutic levels."

The hearing officer's finding that Ms. Binkley failed to seek supervision from Dr. Niaz is not reflective of the appropriate standard of practice. **A collaborative agreement is not an agreement to be supervised.** Collaborative agreements mean that a doctor agrees to be available for questions and referrals, **but not supervision**. The hearing officer's findings of fact indicate that Ms. Binkley and Dr. Niaz were having regular Friday meetings. This is an acceptable practice and the hearing officer did not understand that APNs do not need to be supervised by doctors in order to practice.

With regard to the pregnant patients, the Committee notes that it was documented in the notes that patients were told they should not get pregnant. The documentation indicates that patients were notified that babies will be born addicted. It is an unfortunate position, but an honest one: **weaning a dependent pregnant woman off of controlled substances can be more complicated than weaning a dependent infant.**

The Committee rejects the hearing officer's finding that Ms. Binkley "aided, abetted and/or assisted Dr. Niaz in violations of the Controlled Substances Act." (Hearing officer recommendation at 233)

As noted in the above report, most of the allegations in which this case stood or commenced were nullified by the Joint Commission of the Nursing Licensing Board. This could be because no investigator was sitting on the Joint Commission, and therefore, the decision was not tainted, as it was previously.

The conclusion by the Joint Practice Commission clearly contradicted the finding of the Deliberation Committee and the discovery of the hearing officer, which were written in his "Facts and Findings." The Joint Practice Committee recognized that patients were not seen and examined; that there was no overprescription; and there was no lack of supervision, on which the Deliberation Committee had based their decision. In fact, according to the Joint Commission of the Nursing Board, no such supervision was needed. So the concept of the captain of the ship, on which the Deliberation Committee rested their decision, was utterly baseless. The Joint Practice Committee acknowledged that the law required that the collaborating physician be available for and sufficiently provide consultation.

One of the allegations raised by the hearing officer was that there was no treatment plan in the chart. The Joint Practice Committee effectively showed that the "doctor's orders" written in the chart were proven as the treatment plan. There was no such standard of care that the provider had to write under the heading "Treatment Plan."

The Joint Practice Committee noticed that the hearing officer did not understand how the charts were arranged in the actual practice, as they wrote, "Hearing Officer made them out in his order."

The Joint Practice Committee found the patients were seen every month, which was of high standards. As for the pregnant patients, the Joint Practice Committee disagreed entirely with the approach by the hearing officer and stated, "Weaning a newborn is much safer then weaning a pregnant patient." In fact, the same explanation was given by our defense in the hearing, with references to support those views.

The Joint Practice Committee also found that the side effects of these medications were discussed as mentioned in the charts, which they reviewed, including the risk of these medications on pregnant patients.

One of the significant points highlighted by the Joint Practice Committee was that the patients on Medicaid had limited treatment options available, as most of the long-acting pain medications were very expensive and often denied by Medicaid.

The Joint Practice Commission also rejected the claim by the hearing officer that I failed to coordinate care with other treating providers.

The most critical analysis by the Joint Practice Commission, however, was that the hearing officer improperly acted as a medical expert. The job of a hearing officer was to collect evidence presented at the hearing and, based on those pieces of evidence, conclude the law.

As written in Delaware law:

> [Section] 8735 (v)(1)d, provides that hearing officers have the power to conduct hearings, including any evidentiary hearings. The testimony or evidence so taken or received shall have the same force and effect as if taken or received by the Board or Commission. Upon completion of such Hearing or the taking of such testimony and evidence, the hearing officer shall submit to the Board or Commission findings and recommendations thereon. The findings of fact made by a hearing officer on a complaint are binding upon the Board or Commission, a copy shall be delivered to each of the other parties, who shall have 20 days to submit written exceptions, comments and arguments concerning the conclusions of law and recommended penalty. The Board or Commission shall make its final decision to affirm or modify the hearing officer's recommended conclusions of law and proposed sanctions based upon the written record.

The law clearly indicated the job of the hearing officer, but he acted as an expert, interpreting medical charts and medical treatment and raising allegations that were not raised by the prosecutor. The Joint Practice Commission indicated that the hearing officer did not understand the charts. If he did not understand the charts, the proper action under his task would be to ask for a further explanation during the hearing. *Acting as an expert was another violation of due process by the hearing officer*, which, in my view, only worked to prove the state's side of the story.

This was a good case to see how the licensing board, which, in the eyes of public, was honest, worked for the public, unbiased, and actually conducted their affairs.

In summary, this was a case of (1) violation of due process, (2) violation of a right to a fair trial, (3) discrimination, (4) using a physician as an example to others not to write pain medications, and (5) a strategy to promote agendas and programs for personal or political gain.

Finally, this was also a case of *discrimination*. Why did they select my practice? Both the nurse practitioner and I were faced with the same allegations, same prosecutor, same defense, same experts, and same charts, but the Deliberation Committee concluded almost a 180-degree result for each of us. I reflected significantly on this. It is painful to accept that, in this day and age, discrimination exists. So many doctors in Delaware prescribed pain medication much higher than my practice; they had been prescribing for years but never had disciplinary action against them. Whenever regulating authorities need to make an example of someone, they looked for a person of color, who was considered an easy target.

I recognize that they decided to choose our practice because they thought we were an easy target. We would not have much connection to the licensing board. We would not have the appeal or the support of the mainstream, middle-class population of patients to support us. It is sad to think that despite my education and credentials, the prosecution may have counted on my ethnicity and lack of connections to the type of community they counted on to read the newspaper, and that would allow them to present a case where they would not have to counter strong objections. We were portrayed unfairly in the newspapers and on the internet to a base with whom I did not have multiple connections. Their goal was to make headlines in the newspaper, and they achieved their goal.

The Joint Practice Committee of Nursing Board's conclusion exposed the hearing officer's findings and the Deliberation Committee. How did two results for the same case—one done by the Deliberation Committee for the doctor and the other by the Joint Practice Committee for the nurse practitioner, be totally opposite? Allegations were the same, the hearings were same, conducted together in front of the same hearing officer, but the conclusions were opposite.

If I was the captain of the ship, then they had to prove the nurse practitioner was doing harm or egress medical practice. They had to present deliberation of the nurse practitioner's case before me, as I was labeled as "captain of the ship." They first had to confirm if the ship was really sunk or if it was their illusion. A 1995 movie was titled, *The Englishman Who Went Up a Hill but Came Down a Mountain*. This is an apt description of the proceedings of this case. It was a learning curve to climb the hill. I learned many facets of practice that require routine review, and I will benefit from climbing that hill. Coming down the mountain revealed different revelations. People lose sight of integrity and good intentions. Making an example of me hurt me and my family, friends, practice, and patients. Did I gain insight? Yes. Am I a better practitioner? Yes. However, I was falsely maligned, and throughout this book, I have repeated the issues that I argued, but most were sadly dismissed because of the prosecution's agenda. I am saddened by the lack of fairness. Trust is a cornerstone I build with my patients, and I hope this experience will not taint that objective.

Psalm 106:3 says, "Blessed are they who observe justice, who do righteousness at all times."

The truth is finally revealed, as mentioned in the Quran 17:81: "When the truth is heard against falsehood, falsehood perishes, for falsehood by its nature is bound to perish."

APPENDIX

The amended allegation stated:

- As the nurse practitioners are employed by Respondent in his pain management practice and treat his patients, Respondent is responsible for the prescriptions written by the nurse practitioners and the treatment they render in his office.
- Respondent failed to supervise his office staff properly and adequately, including but not limited to nurse practitioners to ensure that they provided safe, adequate, appropriate, and necessary medical treatment to his patients.
- Respondent failed to properly and adequately train his office staff, including but not limited to nurse practitioners, to ensure that they provided safe, adequate, appropriate, and necessary medical treatment to his patients.
- Beginning in at least 2009, Respondent failed to obtain, evaluate, and document medical histories and physical examinations in the patients' medical records before prescribing controlled substances.
- Beginning in at least 2009, Respondent failed to document in his patients' medical records the nature and intensity of patients' pain, current and past treatments for pain, underlying or coexisting diseases or conditions, the effect of the pain on physical and psychological function, and history of substance abuse.
- Beginning in at least 2009, Respondent failed to document in his patients' medical records the presence of one or more recognized medical indications for the use of a controlled substance.

- Beginning in at least 2009, Respondent failed to document in his patients' medical records written treatment plans stating objectives to be used to determine treatment success, such as pain relief and improved physical and psychosocial function and should indicate if any further diagnostic evaluations or other treatments are planned.
- Beginning in at least 2009, Respondent failed to adjust controlled substances drug therapies to his patients' individual medical needs.
- Beginning in at least 2009, Respondent failed to order other treatment modalities or rehabilitation programs depending on the etiology of the pain and the extent to which the pain is associated with physical and psychosocial impairment.
- Beginning in at least 2009, Respondent failed to discuss the risks and benefits of the use of controlled substances with his patients.
- Beginning in at least 2009, Respondent failed to document in his patients' medical records that he had discussed the risks and benefits of the use of controlled substances with his patients.
- Beginning in at least 2009, Respondent failed to enforce his pain management agreements with patients.
- Beginning in at least 2009, Respondent failed to order appropriate urine/serum medication levels screenings.
- Beginning in at least 2009, Respondent failed to take necessary action including but not limited to discontinuing or decreasing the amount of controlled substances prescribed after urine/serum medication levels screenings indicated that patients were not taking controlled substances medications as prescribed.
- Beginning in at least 2009, Respondent failed to periodically review the course of pain treatment and any new information about the etiology of the pain and patients' State of health.
- Beginning in at least 2009, Respondent failed to evaluated patients' Progress toward treatment objectives, including but not limited to satisfactory response to treatment indicated by decreased pain, increased level function, or improved quality of life.

- Beginning in at least 2009, Respondent failed to assess the appropriateness of continued use of treatment plans that did not result in patient Progress toward treatment objectives.
- Beginning in at least 2009, Respondent failed to refer patients as necessary for additional evaluation and treatment in order to achieve treatment objectives.
- Beginning in at least 2009, Respondent failed to assess, monitor, and/or refer patients at risk for medication misuse, abuse, or diversion.
- Beginning in at least 2009, Respondent failed to keep accurate and complete patient records that included: medical histories and physical examinations; diagnostic, therapeutic and laboratory results; evaluations and consultations; treatment objectives; discussion of risks and benefits; informed patient consents; treatments; medications including the date, type, dosage and quantity prescribed; instructions to patients; agreements with patients; and periodic reviews.
- Beginning in at least 2009, Respondent has prescribed controlled substances to patients in amounts that exceed safe therapeutic levels.
- Beginning in at least 2009, Respondent prescribed controlled substances to patients without conducting proper medical examinations.
- Beginning in at least 2009, Respondent prescribed controlled substances to patients without establishing any legitimate medical basis or need for medication.
- Beginning in at least 2009, Respondent prescribed controlled substances to patients without taking reasonable and necessary precautions to prevent illegal diversion of controlled substances.
- Beginning in at least 2009, Respondent's employee nurse practitioners failed to obtain, evaluate, and document medical histories and physical examinations in the patients' medical records before prescribing controlled substances.

- Beginning in at least 2009, Respondent's employee nurse practitioners, failed to document in patients' medical records the nature and intensity of patients' pain, current and past treatments for pain, underlying or coexisting diseases or conditions, the effect of the pain on physical and psychological function, and history of substance abuse.
- Beginning in at least 20099, Respondent's employee nurse practitioners, failed to document in the patients' medical records the presence of one or more recognized medical indications for the use of a controlled substance.
- Beginning in at least 2009, Respondent's employee nurse practitioners, failed to document in patients' medical records written treatment plans stating objectives to be used to determine treatment success, such as pain relief and improved physical and psychosocial function, and should indicate if any further diagnostic evaluations or other treatment are planned.
- Beginning in at least 2009, Respondent's employee nurse practitioners, failed to adjust controlled substances drug therapies to patients' individual medical needs.
- Beginning in at least 2009, Respondent's employee nurse practitioners failed to order other treatment modalities or rehabilitation programs depending on the etiology of the pain and the extent to which the pain is associated with physical and psychosocial impairment.
- Beginning in at least 2009, Respondent's employee nurse practitioners, failed to discuss the risks and benefits of the use of controlled substances with their patients.
- Beginning in at least 2009, Respondent's employee nurse practitioners, failed to document in patients' medical records that he/she had discussed the risks and benefits of the use of controlled substances with patients.
- Beginning in at least 2009, Respondents employee nurse practitioners, including but not limited to Binkley, failed to enforce written pain management agreements with patients.

- Beginning in at least 2009, Respondent's employee nurse practitioners, ailed to order appropriate urine/serum medication levels screenings.
- Beginning in at least 2009, Respondent's employee nurse practitioners, failed to take necessary action including but not limited to discontinuing or decreasing the amount of controlled substances prescribed after urine/serum medication levels screenings indicated that patients were not taking controlled substances medications as prescribed.
- Beginning in at least 2009, Respondent's employee nurse practitioners failed to periodically review the course of pain treatment and any new information about the etiology of the pain and patients' State of health.
- Beginning in at least 2009, Respondent's employee nurse practitioners, failed to evaluated patients' Progress toward treatment objectives including but not limited to satisfactory response to treatment indicated by decreased pain, increased level of function, or improved quality of life
- Beginning in at least 2009, Respondent's employee nurse practitioners, including but not limited to Binkley, failed to assess the appropriateness of continued use of treatment plans that did not result in patient Progress toward treatment objectives
- Beginning in at least 2009, Respondent's employee nurse practitioners, failed to refer patients as necessary for additional evaluation and treatment in order to achieve treatment objectives.
- Beginning in at least 2009, Respondent's employee nurse practitioners, including but not limited to Binkley, failed to assess, monitor, and/or refer patients at risk for medication misuse, abuse, or diversion.
- Beginning in at least 2009, Respondent's employee nurse practitioners, failed to keep accurate and complete patient records that included: medical histories and physical examinations; diagnostic, therapeutic and laboratory results; evaluations and consultations; treatment objectives; discussion of risks and benefits; informed patient consents; treatments; medications including

133

the date, type, dosage and quantity prescribed; instructions to patients; agreements with patients; and periodic reviews.

- Beginning in at least 2009, Respondent's employee nurse practitioners, including but not limited to Binkley, prescribed controlled substances to patients in amounts that exceed safe therapeutic levels.
- Beginning in at least 2009, Respondent's employee nurse practitioners, including but not limited to Binkley, prescribed controlled substances to patients without conducting proper medical examinations.
- Beginning in at least 2009, Respondent's employee nurse practitioners, including but not limited to Binkley, prescribed controlled substances to patients without establishing any legitimate medical basis or need for medication.
- Beginning in at least 2009, Respondent's employee nurse practitioners, including but not limited to Binkley, prescribed controlled substances to patients without taking reasonable and necessary precautions to prevent illegal diversion of controlled substances.
- Beginning in at least 2009, Respondent and his employee nurse practitioners prescribed controlled substances to pregnant patients without taking necessary and adequate measures to ensure the health and safety of the patients and their unborn children.
- Beginning in at least 2009, as a result of Respondent and his employee nurse practitioners prescribing controlled substances to pregnant patients without taking necessary and adequate measures to ensure the health and safety of the patients and their unborn children, patients' babies were born addicted to controlled substances.
- As a direct or indirect result of the actions and failures to act of Respondent as alleged in paragraphs 6 through 56 herein, his patients suffered physical, psychological, and/or financial harm.
- As a direct or indirect result of the actions and failures to act of Respondent as alleged in paragraphs 6 through 57 herein, patients treated by him and/or his employees died.

- Respondent and his employee nurse practitioners prescribed methadone to patients addicted to heroin.
- Through his misconduct described in paragraphs 6 through 59 herein, Respondent violated the provisions of:

  o 16 Del.C. 4734(a)(7) in that he engaged in conduct inconsistent with the public interest.
  o 16 Del.C. S 4734 (a)(l) and (4) in that he failed to maintain any effective controls to prevent diversion of controlled substances from his office into non-legitimate and illegal channels; and

- Regulation 4.3 of the Uniform Controlled Substances Act Regulations in that he wrote prescriptions for controlled substances to individuals for other than legitimate medical purposes.

Amendment Complaint

Respondent through his conduct alleged in paragraphs 6 through 58 herein, engaged in unprofessional conduct and violated the following provisions of Title 24, Chapter 17:

a. § 1731(b)(l) in that he engaged in unethical practices in connection with the practice of medicine as he violated provisions of the Code of Medical Ethics of the American Medical Association including:

Opinion 9.123 in that his conduct failed to serve his patients' wellbeing while respecting their dignity and rights.

Opinion 10.01 in that he violated his patients' rights: a - to receive information from Respondent and to discuss the benefits, risks, and costs of appropriate treatment alternatives; b - to receive guidance as to the optimal course of action; c - to courtesy, respect, dignity, responsiveness, and timely attention to his or her needs; and

Opinion 10.015 in that he failed to use sound medical judgment, holding the best interests of his patients as paramount.

b. § 1731(b)(3) in that he engaged in dishonorable and unethical conduct likely to harm the public and his patients.

c. § 1731 (b)(6) in that he issued prescriptions for dangerous and/or narcotic drugs, other than for therapeutic or diagnostic purposes.

d. § 1731 (b)(11) in that in prescribing controlled substances to patients in amounts that exceeded safe therapeutic levels, he engaged in misconduct and was incompetent, grossly negligent, and/or engaged in a pattern of negligence in the practice of medicine.

e. § 1731(b)(17) in that he violated provisions of Chapter 17 and the Rules and Regulations of the Board related to medical procedures and the violations more probably than not harmed and/or injured the public and his patients; and

f. § 1731 in that he violated that following Board Rules:

Rule 15.1.4 in that he intentionally failed to maintain records concerning the prescriptions for controlled substances he wrote for his patients.

Rule 15.1.10 in that his conduct has brought discredit upon the medical profession.

Rule 21.1.6 in that he failed to place and follow procedural safeguards to ensure the safe dispensing of drugs at Newark and Elkton; and

Rule 21.1.1 in that he failed to adequately supervise his employee nurse practitioners including but not limited to Binkley and other staff members; and Rule 23 in that he and his employee nurse practitioners prescribed controlled substances to pregnant patients§ 1731(b)(10) and (11) in that he failed to provide adequate supervision to nurse practitioners including but not limited to

Binkley and to other staff members working under his supervision such that his conduct constituted misconduct, incompetence, gross negligence, and/or a pattern of negligence in the practice of medicine.

g. During 2011, Respondent charged and billed patients and/or their insurance companies for larger fees for longer office visits than he and/or his staff provided. Nurse practitioners including but not limited to Binkley and to other staff members working under his supervision such that his conduct constituted misconduct, incompetence, gross negligence, and/or a pattern of negligence in the practice of medicine.

Printed in the United States
by Baker & Taylor Publisher Services